SAMUEL TAYLOR COLERIDGE
Poems selected by JAMES

Samuel Taylor Coleridge (1772–1834) was born in Ottery St Mary, Devon, the youngest son of a clergyman. He was educated at Christ's Hospital School, London, where he began his friendship with Charles Lamb, and Jesus College, Cambridge. He first met Dorothy and William Wordsworth in 1797 and a close association developed between them, issuing in their groundbreaking joint-publication, *Lyrical Ballads*, in 1799. Coleridge subsequently settled in the Lake District, and thereafter in London, where he lectured on Shakespeare and published his literary and philosophical theories in the *Biographia Literaria* (1817). He died in 1834, having overseen a final edition of his *Poetical Works*. As poet, philosopher and critic, Coleridge stands as one of the seminal figures of his time.

James Fenton was born in 1949 and graduated from Magdalen College, Oxford in 1970. His poems were collected in *Terminal Moraine* (1972), *The Memory of War* (1982), *Children in Exile* (1983) and *Out of Danger* (1994). His lectures, delivered as Oxford Professor of Poetry, were collected in *The Strength of Poetry* (2001). *An Introduction to English Poetry* appeared in 2002. His essays on art history were collected in *Leonardo's Nephew* (1998). In 2006 he published his *Selected Poems* and a history of the Royal Academy.

SAMUEL TAYLOR COLERIDGE

Poems selected by

JAMES FENTON

faber and faber

First published in 2006
by Faber and Faber Limited
3 Queen Square London WC1N 3AU

Photoset by RefineCatch Limited, Bungay, Suffolk
Printed in England by Bookmarque Ltd, Croydon, Surrey

The right of James Fenton to be identified as editor
of this work has been asserted in accordance with Section 77
of the Copyright, Designs and Patents Act 1988

A CIP record for this book
is available from the British Library
ISBN 978–0–571–2098–1
      0–571–20981–5

10 9 8 7 6 5 4 3 2 1

Contents

Introduction

The reader of this selection of Coleridge's poems may be surprised that the first items presented should be fragments and drafts rather than finished poems, and that there is such duplication as well: two versions of 'Kubla Khan' and both the verse letter to Sara Hutchinson and the 'Dejection' ode, which Coleridge created as a public version of the private epistle. I would also have put in two versions of 'The Ancient Mariner', given enough space. But is it fair to Coleridge, would it be fair to any poet, to treat his work in this way?

Well, I like Coleridge very much, and I want the reader to like him too, otherwise the whole exercise would be a waste of time. I want the reader to like him for what he is, not for what he fails to be. He is not a perfect poet, in the way that, say, George Herbert is a perfect poet. That is to say, with Herbert you feel that the forms and the language are perfectly congruent with the purposes of the poet. He seems to achieve all that he desires, for he expresses his religious viewpoint in a comprehensive way. His work is all of a piece. It is not problem-strewn. If there were early drafts, one expects that they would point in the direction of the ultimately successful poem, not raise questions about the author's sincerity and purpose, or his veracity. Anyway there are no such drafts, no identifiable juvenilia, no censored passages: all we have is finished work of the highest quality.

Coleridge's poems, by contrast, bring with them all kinds of fascinating doubts. What is finished, and what is unfinished? 'The Pains of Sleep' looks finished, but is said by Coleridge to be a fragment. 'Kubla Khan' certainly looks like a fragment (which is what its author said it was) but has been suspected of being a complete work, cunningly passed off as a fragment. Coleridge's character has been roundly attacked and his veracity impugned, and it may seem naïve to today's reader to accept the story of the 'person on business from Porlock' interrupting the composition of the work. What we are being regaled with, such a reader may feel, is a fable illustrating the workings of inspiration. The Person from Porlock, on this reading, is a fabulous beast.

He has certainly *become* proverbial, as have Xanadu and the Ancient Mariner, the Pleasure Dome and the Albatross. I give two versions of 'Kubla Khan' not because they differ in substance but because the poem takes on a subtly different character when *presented* differently: the first time around, the fragment (as it was privately circulated) seems something of a curiosity to do with the effects of opium; the manuscript appears to have been stuck in an album and valued as an example of the poet's handwriting. By the second version, the text as presented to the public, the poet has evidently become more interested in his own achievement, and, despite his protestation of diffidence, more confident that such a puzzling object could be of interest to the reader. Many years had passed since its composition and the poem had already earned the admiration of Byron, the poet of 'great and deserved celebrity' mentioned in the accompanying note. I would like today's reader to have the chance to think about either way of looking at the poem, and so it is convenient to have both texts with their full apparatus.

The two versions of the 'Dejection' material, by contrast, are very different indeed. The interest here is in the problem that will confront any poet. If I fall in love, am spurned, am loved in return, fall out of love – if any such great common experience befalls me, and I write a poem about it, whom am I addressing? Am I really only addressing the loved one? Or am I speaking to the general public in the guise of speaking to the loved one? If the first, would not my publishing the poem constitute a breach of trust? If the second, would I not be better advised (as a lover) to attend to the actual demands of this supreme relationship, rather than looking, as it were, over my lover's shoulder and addressing the rest of the room?

There are no general answers to these conundrums. If a man or woman is loved by a poet, and receives a poetic epistle, then he or she would be advised to become reconciled to the idea that there is something implicitly public in this form of address. Perhaps that thought will be welcome: the lover is happy and flattered to be chosen as Muse. Perhaps there will only be unease, in which case it might be best for the lover to show a clean pair of heels, to get away before any further damage is done.

From the poet's point of view, it may be possible to move effortlessly to and fro between myself-as-individual and myself-as-representative-man, or it may be hard. At the very least, the poet to whom it always seems insincere to reflect on passion while in passion's throes is going to have a hard time ever producing a love poem. And the poet whose private life is strictly off-limits to his poetry is going to have to work hard to find any subject which inflames him.

Coleridge wrote his verse letter for an intimate circle that included preeminently William and Dorothy Wordsworth. It is not even known whether he sent Sara Hutchinson, the addressee, a copy. He read the first version to William and Dorothy, thereby sharing not only his feelings for Sara but also such quite unprintable emotions as his occasional regrets that he had ever had children:

> Those little Angel Children (woe is me!)
> There have been hours when, feeling how they bind
> And pluck out the Wing-feathers of my Mind,
> Turning my Error to Necessity,
> I have half-wish'd they never had been born!
> *That* seldom! But sad Thought they always bring . . .

These are terrible confessions to make, and they are only a part of the anguished situation evoked by the poem. Coleridge was emotionally estranged from his wife and in love with Sara Hutchinson. Wordsworth was in love with Sara's sister Mary, whom he intended shortly to marry. Before he could do so he had to make a definitive break with his former mistress Annette Vallon, by whom he had a child. Coleridge could encourage Wordsworth to marry Mary, but for himself he could not contemplate divorce. Inextricable from his feelings about his marriage and Wordworth's was a sense that his poetic powers were deserting him.

Between the first composition of the verse letter and the final version of the 'Dejection' ode fall numerous attempts at reusing the material. Coleridge cuts the name Sara and substitutes a fictional Edmund, before turning the work into an address to William (Wordsworth), and publishing it as such, in the *Morning Post*, on Wordsworth's wedding day. Then he reverts to the female figure as addressee, but now she is plain 'Lady'. There were also numerous, no doubt highly edited, showings of the verse letter to different friends, and in one case Coleridge pretended that he had written it for one of his correspondents.

All this radical reshaping of his material may give us a sobering view of the romantic poet as lover, but it is highly characteristic of Coleridge both in his human situation and in his working practice. Whom was he addressing in the first version of the poem? His loved one. With whom was he in love? That's a good question, for he seems in a sense (I do not mean a sexual sense) to have been in love with Wordsworth, or to have been in love with a group that included Wordsworth. He addressed the poem, as written, to Sara Hutchinson, but he *read* it (addressing it in another sense) to William and Dorothy. Then he turned it into a public wedding-present for William and Mary Hutchinson. One way or another, he involved everyone in his plight.

> It was as calm as this, that happy night
> When Mary, thou, & I together were,
> The low decaying Fire our only Light,
> And listen'd to the Stillness of the Air!
> O that affectionate & blameless Maid,

Dear Mary! On her lap my head she lay'd –
  Her Hand was on my Brow,
  Even as my own is now;
And on my Cheek I felt thy eye-lash play.
Such Joy I had, that I may truly say,
My Spirit was awe-stricken with the Excess
And trance-like Depth of it's brief Happiness.

They are listening to the silence together. Mary, who is to marry William, has Coleridge's head on her lap and her hand on his brow. Then he feels Sara's eyelash play on his cheek. And this beatific moment he writes up, and he reads his account to William and Dorothy. This is a poetry that has not yet detached itself from the situation it is decribing: it is pushing matters further.

In choosing to offer the original 1798 text of 'The Ancient Mariner' I am not saying that the later version, with its modernised spelling and marginal annotations, ruins the original idea. I am simply imagining that the reader may well own some other book with the more conventional text. The earlier version is nearer the original idea for the poem: that it be a ballad written in the old English style, as found in collections of early verse such as Percy's *Reliques*. The poet Anna Letitia Barbauld told Coleridge, perhaps soon after its first publication, that 'the only faults she found with the Ancient Mariner were – that it was improbable, and had no moral.'

Coleridge's reply to these criticisms, which would have been common at the time, is rightly held to be a key to his aesthetic:

As for the probability – to be sure that might admit some question – but I told her that in my judgment the chief fault of the poem was that it had too much moral, and that too openly obtruded on the reader. It ought to have had no more moral than the story of the merchant sitting down to eat dates by the side of a well and throwing the shells aside, and the Genii starting up and saying he must kill the merchant, because a date shell had put out the eye of the Genii's son.

In another account of the same incident, Coleridge says to Mrs Barbauld, whose intentions had been complimentary, that

the only fault in the poem is that there is *too much* [of a moral]! In a work of such pure imagination I ought not to have stopped to give reasons for things, or inculcate humanity to beasts. The 'Arabian Nights' might have taught me better.

And he goes on to retail the same story.

The reply to Mrs Barbauld is very spirited, and it might just as appropriately have been made to Wordsworth who, having first printed 'The Ancient Mariner' in *Lyrical Ballads*, later appended a note acknowledging that many people had been 'much displeased' with the poem and that Coleridge had wanted it suppressed. Wordworth goes on:

The Poem of my Friend has indeed great defects; first, that the principal person has no distinct character, either in his profession of Mariner, or as a human being who having been long under the control of supernatural impressions might be supposed to partake of something supernatural: secondly, that he does not act, but is continually acted upon: thirdly, that the events having no necessary connection do not produce each other; and lastly, that the imagery is somewhat too laboriously accumulated.

With egregious complacency, Wordsworth congratulates himself on having nevertheless refused to suppress the 'Ancient Mariner' by dropping it from *Lyrical Ballads*.

The complaint that the Mariner does not act but is acted upon reminds us of another unfair *obiter dictum*: Yeats's 'passive suffering is not a theme for poetry'. Indeed it is the same capricious objection. As it happens the Mariner does act: he shoots the Albatross, and this action, like the throwing of the date shell, involves him in a guilt that he could not have predicted, for there is no way that the merchant could have known that throwing date shells aside might cause the death of a genie's son (in the original story, the son has been killed, which is why the merchant must die).

The action is the starting point of the story. In Coleridge's view it is not to be questioned. It is something that happens, in the idiom of such stories. Neither the merchant, nor his wife, nor anyone else who hears about it doubts that the merchant has indeed caused the son's death. It is one of the givens of the story, which is a creation of 'pure imagination'. And that is also what, incidentally, 'Kubla Khan' might be thought to be. And I have often wondered whether the surprisingly long time Coleridge took to bring that 'fragment' before the public might not have been the result of some initial discouragement by William and Dorothy Wordsworth.

Still, Coleridge in his sly way managed to deal with many of the problems that beset him, and there is no possibility of reaching back into the past to help him out of those difficulties we do not think he solved in the best possible fashion. Printing the first version of the 'Ancient Mariner' enables us to preface the poem with the simple, geographically matter-of-fact 'Argument' in its original form, before the poet pointed up the mariner's guilt in the revised version of 1800:

> How a Ship, having first sailed to the Equator, was driven
> by Storms to the cold Country towards the South Pole; how
> the Ancient Mariner cruelly and in contempt of the laws of
> hospitality killed a Sea-bird and how he was followed by
> many and strange Judgements: and in what manner he
> came back to his own country.

If one approached the Arabian Nights story in this spirit, one would say that the merchant, cruelly and in contempt of the ancient anti-litter laws, threw away some date shells, thereby killing the Genie's son. If the Mariner was being punished for cruelty to animals, what are we to say of the deity who kills the whole ship's crew, in order to underline His point?

This selection of Coleridge is perhaps the first to be able to rely on the monumental Variorum text edited by J. C. C. Mays, and I am extremely grateful for Professor Mays's permission to draw on his work. His text, which comes in four volumes, is the kind that most people would only want to consult in libraries. But any student of Coleridge who is trying to make a serious point in detail about any Coleridge poem will do well to use the Mays edition, since all previous texts are marred by odd little misreadings, on which the writer will have to take a view. For instance, in the description of the Netherlands, given here as item 11, Mays has 'The fly-transfixing Spires' where others have made us accustomed to 'The sky-transfixing Spires'. The Mays version may seem crazy, but we have to square up to it if that is what is in the manuscript. In item 12, the last line used to read 'Her loss was to my heart, like the heart-blood.' This made it seem as if the speaker in the poem was living off his sense of loss. 'Her Love was to my Heart, like the Heart-blood' makes a very important change.

Here are some 'tasting notes' on the fragments:

Item 1. Called by Mays 'Lines Written in a Dream', it evokes what is now called clinical depression. A characteristic Coleridge theme, in a nutshell.

Item 2. A cushat or cushit: a pigeon or ring-dove in North Country and Borders dialect. Mallarmé's advice to Degas, that poems are not made out of ideas but out of words, comes to mind. This is what a poem looks like in the egg.

Item 3. A line-and-a-half, from the notebooks, waiting for inclusion in 'Frost at Midnight'. This is how lines occur.

Item 4. Here is Coleridge 'borrowing' a good line from his extensive reading. The second line comes from Fulke Greville. The nineteenth century is here reading the seventeenth. The result is like a motto from an emblem book.

Item 5. Mays quotes the third stanza of the Percy ballad 'Waly, Waly, Love be bonny':

Marti'mas wind, when wilt thou blaw
   And shake the green leaves aff the tree?
O gentle death, whan wilt thou cum?
   For of my life I am wearìe.

Line three in the Coleridge stanza is the one that dates it to the Romantic period.

Item 6. As Mays says, this reads like a fragment of a blank-verse drama. But the notebook page on which it is written is marked with anagrams and initials indicating that the situation in the fragment derives from the relationship between Wordworth and Coleridge and the women in their lives. A dramatic suicide threat.

Item 7. Another 'dramatic' line, but why? Because we do not think of Coleridge as vengeful and glorying in it? But here he is meditating on how to describe a spectacular revenge.

Item 8. Given the title 'Bo-Peep and I Spy', it is a sort of poem Coleridge thought appropriate 'For *Autographs*' – something to write on a page of an album. It illustrates the affinity between poetry and play.

Item 9. A song. Another poem for the autograph book. The unpleasant thought that love conceals a sword within a wreath of myrtle comes from a Greek tradition, which has Harmodius and Aristogeiton kill the younger brother of the Athenian tyrant Hippias, concealing their swords in this way.

Item 10. Characteristic of Coleridge's fascination with weather effects, these lines derive from his reading of Jean Paul.

Item 11. A description of the Netherlands. 'The fly-transfixing Spires' noted above. Previous editors thought they must be sky-transfixing.

Item 12. He's thinking in Italian grammar. 'Nor . . . Have I, to whom' – '*Non ho cui*'.

Item 13. An epigraph. Acknowledges conflict between the pull of Truth and that of Imagination (Fancy).

Item 14. He's thinking in Latin, perhaps. Depression again.

Item 15. 'Lines on Looking Seaward' – ornithological sketch.

Item 16. These 'Studies in Cloud Effects' are a poet's equivalent to Constable's oil sketches of clouds.

Item 17. Another characteristic oil sketch.

Item 18. Nature mythologised. A 'deep romantic Chasm' with Yew instead of 'Cedarn' cover.

Item 19. One for the autograph book . . .

James Fenton

SAMUEL TAYLOR COLERIDGE

[1]

I know tis but a Dream, yet feel more anguish
Than if 'twere Truth. It has been often so,
Must I die under it? Is no one near?
Will no one hear these stifled groans, & wake me?

[2]

Or wren or linnet
In Bush and Bushet:
No tree, but in it
A cooing Cushit.

[3]

The reed roof'd Village still bepatch'd with snow
Smok'd in the sun-thaw.

[4]

Let Eagles bid the Tortoise sunward soar –
As vainly Strength speaks to a broken mind.

[5]

Come, come, thou bleak December Wind,
And blow the dry Leaves from the Tree!
Flash, like a Love-thought, thro' me, Death
And take a Life, that wearies me.

[6]

           I have experienc'd
The worst, the World can wreak on me; the worst
That can make Life indifferent, yet disturb
With whisper'd Discontents the dying prayer.
I have beheld the whole of all, wherein
My Heart had any interest in this Life,
To be disrent and torn from off my Hopes,
That nothing now is left. Why then live on?
That Hostage, which the world had in it's keeping
Given by me as a Pledge that I would live,
That Hope of Her, say rather, that pure Faith
In her fix'd Love, which held me to keep truce
With the Tyranny of Life – is gone ah whither?
What boots it to reply? – 'tis gone! and now
Well may I break this Pact, this League, of Blood
That ties me to myself – and break I shall' –

[7]

A sumptuous and magnificent revenge.

[8]

'In the corner *one* –
   I Spy, Love!
'In the corner *none* –
   I spy, Love.

4

[9]

Tho' hid in spiral myrtle Wreath,
Love is a sword that cuts its Sheath:
And thro' the Slits, itself has made,
We spy the Glitter of the Blade.

But thro' the Slits, itself had made,
We spy no less too, that the Blade
Is eat away or snapt atwain,
And nought but Hilt and Stump remain.

[10]

(A)
A low dead Thunder muttered thro' the Night,
As twere a Giant angry in his Sleep –

(B)
Nature! sweet Nurse! O take me in thy Lap –
And tell me of my Father yet unseen
Sweet Tales & True, that lull me into Sleep,
& leave me dreaming. –

(C)
The Day of our dire Fate as yet but dawns,
These Tears the bright Drops of the morning Rainbow
Foretelling Tempest! –

[11]

Water and Windmills, Greenness, Islets Green,
Willows whose trunks beside the Shadows stood
Of their own higher half, and willowy Swamps,

Farm-houses that at anchor seemed & on the inland sky
The fly-transfixing Spires –
Water, wide water, greenness & green banks
And water seen

[12]

I stand alone, nor tho' my Heart should break
Have I, to whom I may complain or speak.
Here I stand, a hopeless man and sad
Who hoped to have seen my Love, my Life.
And strange it were indeed, could I be glad
Remembring her, my Soul's betrothed Wife/
For in this World no creature, that has life,
Was e'er to me so gracious & so good/
Her Love was to my Heart, like the Heart-blood.

[13]

Truth I pursued, as Fancy sketch'd the way,
And wiser men than I went worse astray.

[14]

O mercy! O me miserable man!
Slowly my Wisdom, & how slowly comes
My Virtue! and how rapidly pass off
My Joys, my Hopes, my Friendships, & my Love!

[15]

Seaward, white-gleaming thro' the busy Scud
With arching Wings the Sea-mew o'er my head
Posts on, as bent on speed; now passaging
Edges the stiffer Breeze, now yielding *drifts*,
Now floats upon the Air, and sends from far
A wildly-wailing Note.

[16]

(A)

Twas not a mist, nor was it quite a cloud,
But it pass'd smoothly on towards the Sea
Smoothly & lightly betwixt Earth & Heaven.

(B)

                    So thin a cloud –
It scarce bedimm'd the Star that shone behind it.

(C)

                    And Hesper now
Paus'd on the welkin's blue & cloudless brink,
A golden circlet! while the Star of Jove,
That other lovely Star, high o'er my head
Shone whitely in the center of his Haze.

(D)

            – one black-blue Cloud
Stretched, like the heavens o'er all the cope of Heaven

Over the broad tho' shallow, rapid Stream,
The Alder, a vast hollow Trunk, & ribb'd
Within/ all mossy green with mosses manifold,
And Ferns still waving in the river breeze,
Sent out, like Fingers, 7 projecting Trunks,
The shortest twice 6 of a tall man's Strides,
One curving upward, and in it's middle growth
Rose straight with grove of Twigs, a pollard Tree,
The rest more brookward, gradual in descent,
One on the Brook, & one befoam'd it's waters,
One ran along the bank, with elk-like Head
And pomp of Antlers/ – but still that one
That lay upon or just above the brook
And straight across it, more than halfway o'er
Ends in a broad broad head, & a white Thorn
Thicket of Twigs – & here another Tree
As if the winds & waves had work'd by art
That it, with similar Head, & similar Thicket
Bridging the Stream compleat/ thro' these two Thickets
The Shepherd Lads had cut & plan'd a Path/
O sweet in summer/ & in winter Storms
I have cross'd the same unharm'd.

O'er hung with Yew, midway the Muses' Mount,
From thy sweet murmur far, O Hippocrene,
Turbid and black upboils an angry fount
Tossing it's shatter'd foam in vengeful spleen:
Phlegethon's Rage, Cocytus' wailings hoarse
Alternate now, now mixt, make known it's headlong
    course.

Thither with terror stricken and surprize
(For sure such Haunts were ne'er the Muses' Choice)
Euterpe led me; mute with asking eyes
I stood expectant of her heavenly race –
Her Voice entranc'd my terror and made flow
In a rude Understrain the maniac fount below.

Whene'er (the Goddess said) abhorr'd of Jove
Usurping Power his hands in blood imbues,
And

[19] Kubla Khan

[Coleridge's fair copy – BM Add MS 50847]

In Xannadù did Cubla Khan
A stately Pleasure-Dome decree;
Where Alph, the sacred River, ran
Thro' Caverns measureless to Man
Down to a sunless Sea.
So twice six miles of fertile ground
With Walls and Towers were compass'd round:
And here were Gardens bright with sinuous Rills
Where blossom'd many an incense-bearing Tree,
And here were Forests ancient as the Hills
Enfolding sunny Spots of Greenery.
But o! that deep romantic Chasm, that slanted
Down a green Hill athwart a cedarn Cover,
A savage Place, as holy and inchanted
As e'er beneath a waning Moon was haunted
By Woman wailing for her Daemon Lover:
From forth this Chasm with hideous Turmoil seething,
As if this Earth in fast thick Pants were breathing,
A mighty Fountain momently was forc'd,
Amid whose swift half-intermitted Burst
Huge Fragments vaulted like rebounding Hail,
Or chaffy Grain beneath the Thresher's Flail:
And mid these dancing Rocks at once & ever
It flung up momently the sacred River.
Five miles meandring with a mazy Motion
Thro' Wood and Dale the sacred River ran,
Then reach'd the Caverns measureless to Man
And sank in Tumult to a lifeless Ocean;
And mid this Tumult Cubla heard from far
Ancestral Voices prophesying War.
       The Shadow of the Dome of Pleasure
       Floated midway on the Wave

Where was heard the mingled Measure
From the Fountain and the Cave.
It was a miracle of rare Device,
A sunny Pleasure-Dome with Caves of Ice!

A Damsel with a Dulcimer
In a Vision once I saw:
It was an Abyssinian Maid,
And on her Dulcimer she play'd
Singing of Mount Amara.
Could I revive within me
Her Symphony & Song,
To such deep Delight 'twould win me,
That with Music loud and long
I would build that Dome in Air,
That sunny Dome! Those Caves of Ice!
And all, who heard, should see them there,
And all should cry, Beware! Beware!
His flashing Eyes! his floating Hair!
Weave a circle round him thrice,
And close your eyes in holy Dread:
For He on Honey-dew hath fed
And drank the Milk of Paradise.

This fragment with a good deal more, not recoverable, composed, in a
sort of Reverie brought on by two grains of Opium, taken to check a dysen-
tery, at a Farm House between Porlock & Linton, a quarter of a mile from
Culbone Church, in the fall of the year, 1797.   S. T. Coleridge

[20] Kubla Khan, or a Vision in a Dream

OF THE FRAGMENT OF KUBLA KHAN
The following fragment is here published at the request of a poet of great and deserved celebrity, and as far as the Author's own opinions are concerned, rather as a psychological curiosity, than on the ground of any supposed *poetic* merits.

In the summer of the year 1797, the Author, then in ill health, had retired to a lonely farm-house between Porlock and Linton, on the Exmoor confines of Somerset and Devonshire. In consequence of a slight indisposition, an anodyne had been prescribed, from the effects of which he fell asleep in his chair at the moment that he was reading the following sentence, or words of the same substance, in 'Purchas's Pilgrimage:' 'Here the Khan Kubla commanded a palace to be built, and a stately garden thereunto. And thus ten miles of fertile ground were inclosed with a wall.' The author continued for about three hours in a profound sleep, at least of the external senses, during which time he has the most vivid confidence, that he could not have composed less than from two to three hundred lines; if that indeed can be called composition in which all the images rose up before him as *things*, with a parallel production of the correspondent expressions, without any sensation or consciousness of effort. On awaking he appeared to himself to have a distinct recollection of the whole, and taking his pen, ink, and paper, instantly and eagerly wrote down the lines that are here preserved. At this moment he was unfortunately called out by a person on business from Porlock, and detained by him above an hour, and on his return to his room, found to his no small surprise and mortification, that though he still retained some vague and dim recollection of the general purpose of the vision, yet, with the exception of some eight or ten scattered lines and images, all the rest had passed away like the images on the surface of a stream into which a stone has been cast, but, alas! without the after restoration of the latter:

> Then all the charm
> Is broken – all that phantom-world so fair
> Vanishes, and a thousand circlets spread,
> And each mis-shape the other. Stay awhile,
> Poor youth! who scarcely dar'st lift up thine eyes –
> The stream will soon renew its smoothness, soon

The visions will return! And lo, he stays,
And soon the fragments dim of lovely forms
Come trembling back, unite, and now once more
The pool becomes a mirror.

Yet from the still surviving recollections in his mind, the Author has frequently purposed to finish for himself what had been originally, as it were, given to him. Αὔριον ἄδιον ἄσω: but the to-morrow is yet to come.

As a contrast to this vision, I have annexed a fragment of a very different character, describing with equal fidelity the dream of pain and disease.

In Xanadu did KUBLA KHAN
A stately pleasure-dome decree:
Where ALPH, the sacred river, ran
Through caverns measureless to man
   Down to a sunless sea.
So twice five miles of fertile ground
With walls and towers were girdled round;
And here were gardens bright with sinuous rills
Where blossom'd many an incense-bearing tree;
And here were forests ancient as the hills,
Enfolding sunny spots of greenery.

But oh that deep romantic chasm which slanted
Down the green hill athwart a cedarn cover!
A savage place! as holy and inchanted
As e'er beneath a waning moon was haunted
By woman wailing for her demon-lover!
And from this chasm, with ceaseless turmoil seething,
As if this earth in fast thick pants were breathing,
A mighty fountain momently was forced:
Amid whose swift half-intermitted Burst
Huge fragments vaulted like rebounding hail,
Or chaffy grain beneath the thresher's flail:
And mid these dancing rocks at once and ever
It flung up momently the sacred river.
Five miles meandering with a mazy motion

Through wood and dale the sacred river ran,
Then reached the caverns measureless to man,
And sank in tumult to a lifeless ocean:
And 'mid this tumult Kubla heard from far
Ancestral voices prophesying war!

   The shadow of the dome of pleasure
   Floated midway on the waves;
   Where was heard the mingled measure
   From the fountain and the caves.

It was a miracle of rare device,
A sunny pleasure-dome with caves of ice!

   A damsel with a dulcimer
   In a vision once I saw:
   It was an Abyssinian maid
   And on her dulcimer she play'd,
   Singing of Mount Abora.
   Could I revive within me
   Her symphony and song,
   To such a deep delight 'twould win me,
That with music loud and long,
I would build that dome in air,
That sunny dome! those caves of ice!
And all who heard should see them there,
And all should cry, Beware! Beware!
His flashing eyes, his floating hair!
Weave a circle round him thrice,
And close your eyes with holy dread:
For he on honey-dew hath fed,
And drank the milk of Paradise.

[21] The Pains of Sleep

Ere on my bed my limbs I lay,
It hath not been my use to pray
With moving lips or bended knees;
But silently, by slow degrees,
My spirit I to Love compose,
In humble Trust mine eye-lids close,
With reverential resignation,
No wish conceived, no thought expressed!
Only a *sense* of supplication,
A sense o'er all my soul imprest
That I am weak, yet not unblest,
Since in me, round me, every where
Eternal Strength and Wisdom are.

But yester-night I pray'd aloud
In anguish and in agony,
Up-starting from the fiendish crowd
Of shapes and thoughts that tortured me:
A lurid light, a trampling throng,
Sense of intolerable wrong,
And whom I scorn'd, those only strong!
Thirst of revenge, the powerless will
Still baffled, and yet burning still!
Desire with loathing strangely mixed
On wild or hateful objects fixed.
Fantastic passions! mad'ning brawl!
And shame and terror over all!
Deeds to be hid which were not hid,
Which all confused I could not know,
Whether I suffered, or I did:
For all seemed guilt, remorse or woe,
My own or others still the same
Life-stifling fear, soul-stifling shame!

So two nights passed: the night's dismay
Sadden'd and stunn'd the coming day.
Sleep, the wide blessing, seemed to me
Distemper's worst calamity.
The third night, when my own loud scream
Had waked me from the fiendish dream,
O'ercome with sufferings strange and wild,
I wept as I had been a child;
And having thus by tears subdued
My anguish to a milder mood,
Such punishments, I said, were due
To natures deepliest stain'd with sin:
For aye entempesting anew
Th' unfathomable hell within
The horror of their deeds to view,
To know and loathe, yet wish and do!
Such griefs with such men well agree,
But wherefore, wherefore fall on me?
To be beloved is all I need,
And whom I love, I love indeed.

[22] Christabel

PREFACE

The first part of the following poem was written in the year 1797, at Stowey, in the county of Somerset. The second part, after my return from Germany, in the year 1800, at Keswick, Cumberland. It is probable, that if the poem had been finished at either of the former periods, or if even the first and second part had been published in the year 1800, the impression of its originality would have been much greater than I dare at present expect. But for this, I have only my own indolence to blame. The dates are mentioned for the exclusive purpose of precluding charges of plagiarism or servile imitation from myself. For there is amongst us a set of critics, who seem to hold, that every possible thought and image is traditional; who have no notion that there are such things as fountains in the world, small as well as great; and who would therefore charitably derive every rill they behold flowing, from a perforation made in some other man's tank. I am confident, however, that as far as the present poem is concerned, the celebrated poets whose writings I might be suspected of having imitated, either in particular passages, or in the tone and the spirit of the whole, would be among the first to vindicate me from the charge, and who, on any striking coincidence, would permit me to address them in this doggerel version of two monkish Latin hexameters.

'Tis mine and it is likewise yours;
But an if this will not do;
Let it be mine, good friend! for I
Am the poorer of the two.

I have only to add, that the metre of the Christabel is not, properly speaking, irregular, though it may seem so from its being founded on a new principle: namely, that of counting in each line the accents, not the syllables. Though the latter may vary from seven to twelve, yet in each line the accents will be found to be only four. Nevertheless this occasional variation in number of syllables is not introduced wantonly, or for the mere ends of convenience, but in correspondence with some transition, in the nature of the imagery or passion.

PART I

Tis the middle of Night by the Castle Clock,
And the Owls have awaken'd the crowing Cock:

Tu-u-whoo! Tu-u-whoo!
And hark, again! the crowing Cock,
How drowsily it crew.

Sir Leoline, the Baron rich,
Hath a toothless mastiff Bitch:
From her Kennel beneath the Rock
She maketh Answer to the Clock,
Four for the Quarters and twelve for the Hour,
Ever and aye, by Shine and Shower,
Sixteen short Howls, not overloud;
Some say, she sees my Lady's Shroud.

Is the Night chilly and dark?
The Night is chilly but not dark.
The thin grey Cloud is spread on high,
It covers but not hides the Sky.
The Moon is behind, and at the Full,
And yet she looks both small and dull.
The Night is chill, the Cloud is grey:
Tis a Month before the Month of May,
And the Spring comes slowly up this way.

The lovely Lady, Christabel,
Whom her Father loves so well,
What makes her in the Wood so late
A furlong from the Castle Gate?
She had dreams all yesternight
Of her own betrothed Knight,
And She in the Midnight Wood will pray
For the Weal of her Lover, that's far away.

She stole along, She nothing spoke,
The Sighs she heav'd, were soft and low,
And nought was green upon the Oak,
But Moss and rarest Misletoe:
She kneels beneath the huge Oak Tree,
And in Silence prayeth She.

The Lady sprang up suddenly,
The lovely Lady, Christabel!
It moan'd as near, as near can be,
But what it is, She cannot tell –
On the other Side it seems to be
Of the huge broad-breasted old Oak Tree.

The Night is chill; the Forest bare;
Is it the Wind that moaneth bleak?
There is not Wind enough in the Air
To move away the ringlet Curl
From the lovely Lady's Cheek –
There is not Wind enough to twirl
The One red Leaf, the last of its Clan,
That dances as often as dance it can,
Hanging so light and hanging so high
On the topmost Twig that looks up at the Sky.

Hush, beating Heart of Christabel!
Jesu Maria, shield her well!

She folded her Arms beneath her Cloak,
And stole to the other side of the Oak.
    What sees She there?

There She sees a Damsel bright
Drest in a silken Robe of White;
That shadowy in the moonlight shone:
The Neck, that made that white robe wan,
Her stately Neck and Arms were bare;
Her blue-vein'd Feet unsandal'd were;
And wildly glitter'd here and there
The Gems entangled in her Hair.
I guess, 'twas frightful there to see
A Lady so richly clad, as She,
    Beautiful exceedingly!

'Mary Mother, save me now!'
Said Christabel 'And who art thou?'

The Lady strange made Answer meet,
And her Voice was faint and sweet:
'Have Pity on my sore Distress,
I scarce can speak for Weariness.
Stretch forth thy Hand, and have no fear –'

Said Christabel, 'How cam'st thou here?'
And the Lady, whose Voice was faint and sweet,
Did thus pursue her answer meet.

'My Sire is of a noble Line,
And my Name is Geraldine.
Five Warriors seiz'd me yestermorn,
Me, even me, a Maid forlorn;
They chok'd my Cries with Force and Fright,
And tied me on a Palfrey white;
The Palfrey was as fleet as Wind,
And they rode furiously behind.
They spurr'd amain, their Steeds were white,
And once we cross'd the Shade of Night.
As sure as Heaven shall rescue me,
I have no Thought what Men they be,
Nor do I know how long it is
(For I have lain entranc'd, I wis)
Since One, the tallest of the five,
Took me from the Palfrey's Back,
A weary Woman scarce alive.
Some mutter'd Words his Comrades spoke,
He plac'd me underneath this Oak,
He swore they would return with haste;
Whither they went, I cannot tell –
I thought I heard, some minutes past,
Sounds as of a Castle Bell.

Stretch forth thy Hand (thus ended She)
And help a wretched Maid to flee.'

Then Christabel stretcht forth her Hand
And comforted fair Geraldine:
'O well, bright Dame! may you command
The Service of Sir Leoline –
And gladly our stout Chivalry
Will he send forth and friends withal
To guide and guard you, safe and free,
Home to your noble Father's Hall.'

She rose, and forth with steps they pass'd,
That strove to be, and were not fast.
Her gracious Stars the Lady blest,
And thus spake on sweet Christabel –
'All our Household are at rest,
The Hall as silent as the Cell;
Sir Leoline is weak in health,
And may not well awaken'd be;
But we will move as if in stealth,
And I beseech your Courtesy
This Night to share your Couch with me.'

They cross'd the Moat, and Christabel
Took the Key that fitted well;
A little Door she open'd straight
All in the middle of the Gate,
The Gate, that was iron'd within and without,
Where an Army in Battle Array had march'd out.

The Lady sank, belike thro' Pain,
And Christabel with Might and Main
Lifted her up, a weary Weight,
Over the Threshold of the Gate:
Then the Lady rose again,
And mov'd, as She were not in Pain.

So free from Danger, free from Fear
They cross'd the Court: right glad they were.
And Christabel devoutly cried
To the Lady by her side,
'Praise we the Virgin all divine
Who hath rescued thee from thy Distress!'
'Alas, alas!' said Geraldine,
'I cannot speak for Weariness.'
So free from Danger, free from Fear,
They cross'd the Court: right glad they were.

Outside her Kennel the Mastiff old
Lay fast asleep in Moonshine cold.
The Mastiff old did not awake,
Yet she an angry moan did make.
And what can ail the Mastiff Bitch?
Never till now she utter'd Yell
Beneath the eye of Christabel.
Perhaps, it is the Owlet's Scritch:
For what can ail the Mastiff Bitch?

They pass'd the Hall, that echoes still
Pass as lightly as you will.
The Brands were flat, the Brands were dying
Amid their own white Ashes lying;
But when the Lady pass'd, there came
A Tongue of Light, a Fit of Flame,
And Christabel saw the Lady's Eye,
And nothing else saw she thereby
Save the Boss of the Shield of Sir Leoline tall,
Which hung in a murky old Nitch in the Wall.
'O softly tread,' said Christabel,
'My Father seldom sleepeth well.'

Sweet Christabel her feet doth bare,
And jealous of the list'ning Air,
They steal their way from stair to stair,

Now in Glimmer, and now in Gloom,
And now they pass the Baron's Room,
As still as Death with stifled Breath!
And now have reach'd her Chamber Door,
And now doth Geraldine press down
The Rushes of the Chamber Floor.

The Moon shines dim in th' open Air,
And not a Moonbeam enters here.
But they without its Light can see
The Chamber carv'd so curiously,
Carv'd with figures strange and sweet
All made out of the Carver's Brain
For a Lady's Chamber meet:
The Lamp with twofold silver Chain
Is fasten'd to an Angel's Feet.

The silver Lamp burns dead and dim;
But Christabel the Lamp will trim –
She trimm'd the Lamp, and made it bright,
And left it swinging to and fro,
While Geraldine in wretched Plight
Sank down upon the Floor below.

'O weary Lady, Geraldine,
I pray you, drink this cordial Wine.
It is a Wine of virtuous powers,
My Mother made it of wild Flowers.'

'And will your Mother pity me,
Who am a Maiden most forlorn?'

Christabel answer'd – 'Woe is me!
She died the hour, that I was born.
I have heard the grey-hair'd Friar tell,
How on her Death-bed she did say
That she should hear the Castle Bell
Strike twelve upon my Wedding Day.

O Mother dear! that thou wert here!'
'I would,' said Geraldine, 'She were!'

But soon with alter'd Voice said She –
'Off, wandering Mother! Peak and pine!
I have power to bid thee flee.'
Alas! what ails poor Geraldine?
Why stares she with unsettled Eye?
Can she the bodiless Dead espy?
And why with hollow Voice cries she,
'Off, Woman, off! this Hour is mine –
Though thou her Guardian Spirit be,
Off, Woman, off! tis given to me.'

Then Christabel knelt by the Lady's Side,
And rais'd to heaven her eyes so blue –
'Alas,' said she, 'this ghastly Ride –
Dear Lady! it hath wilder'd you!'
The Lady wip'd her moist cold brow,
And faintly said, 'Tis over now!'

Again the wild flower Wine she drank,
Her fair large Eyes 'gan glitter bright,
And from the Floor, whereon she sank,
The lofty Lady stood upright:
She was most beautiful to see,
Like a Lady of a far Countreè.

And thus the lofty Lady spake –
'All they, who live in th' upper Sky,
Do love you, holy Christabel!
And you love them, and for their sake
And for the Good which me befel,
Even I in my Degree will try,
Fair Maiden, to requite you well.
But now unrobe yourself: for I
Must pray, ere yet in bed I lie.'

24

Quoth Christabel, 'So let it be!'
And as the Lady bade, did she.
Her gentle Limbs did she undress,
And lay down in her Loveliness.

But thro' her Brain of Weal and Woe
So many Thoughts mov'd to and fro,
That vain it were her lids to close;
So half way from the Bed she rose,
And on her Elbow did recline
To look at the Lady Geraldine.

Beneath the Lamp the Lady bow'd
And slowly roll'd her eyes around,
Then drawing in her Breath aloud,
Like one that shudder'd, she unbound
The Cincture from beneath her Breast:
Her silken Robe and inner Vest
Dropt to her feet, and fell in View,
Behold! her Bosom and half her Side –
A Sight to dream of, not to tell!
O shield her! shield sweet Christabel!

Yet Geraldine nor speaks nor stirs;
Ah! what a stricken Look was hers!
Deep from within she seems half-way
To lift some weight, with sick Assay,
And eyes the Maid and seeks delay:
Then suddenly as one defied
Collects herself in scorn and pride
And lay down by the Maiden's side:
And in her arms the Maid she took,
    Ah weladay!
And with low Voice and doleful Look
These Words did say:

'In the Touch of this Bosom there worketh a Spell,
Which is Lord of thy Utterance, Christabel!

Thou knowest to night and wilt know tomorrow
This Mark of my Shame, this Seal of my Sorrow;
  But vainly thou warrest,
  For this is alone in
  Thy Power to declare,
  That in the dim Forest
  Thou heard'st a low Moaning,
And found'st a bright Lady, surpassingly fair.
And didst bring her home with thee in Love and in Charity
To shield her and shelter her from the damp Air.'

THE CONCLUSION TO PART I

It was a lovely Sight to see
The Lady Christabel, when She
Was praying at the old Oak Tree.
  Amid the jagged Shadows
  Of mossy leafless Boughs
  Kneeling in the Moonlight
  To make her gentle Vows;
Her slender Palms together prest,
Heaving sometimes on her Breast;
Her Face resign'd to Bliss or Bale –
Her Face, Oh call it fair not pale,
And both blue Eyes more bright than clear,
Each about to have a Tear.

With open eyes (ah woe is me!)
Asleep, and dreaming fearfully,
Fearfully dreaming, yet, I wis,
Dreaming that alone, which is –
O Sorrow and Shame! Can this be She,
The Lady, who knelt at the old Oak Tree?
And lo! the Worker of these Harms,
That holds the Maiden in her Arms,
Seems to slumber still and mild,
As a Mother with her Child.

A Star hath set, a Star hath risen,
O Geraldine! since Arms of thine
Have been the lovely Lady's Prison.
O Geraldine! One Hour was thine –
Thou'st had thy Will! By Tairn and Rill
The Night-birds all that Hour were still.
But now they are jubilant anew,
From Cliff and Tower, Tu-whoo! Tu-whoo!
Tu-whoo! tu-whoo! from Wood and Fell!

And see! the Lady Christabel
Gathers herself from out her Trance;
Her Limbs relax, her Countenance
Grows sad and soft; the smooth thin Lids
Close o'er her Eyes; and Tears she sheds –
Large Tears, that leave the Lashes bright!
And oft the while she seems to smile
As Infants at a sudden Light!

Yea, she doth smile and she doth weep,
Like a youthful Hermitess
Beauteous in a Wilderness,
Who, praying always, prays in Sleep.

And if she move unquietly,
Perchance, tis but the Blood so free
Comes back and tingles in her Feet.
No doubt, she hath a Vision sweet.
What if her guardian Spirit twere?
What if She knew her Mother near?
But this she knows, in Joys and Woes,
That Saints will aid if Men will call,
For the blue Sky bends over all!

PART II

Each matin Bell, the Baron saith,
Knells us back to a World of Death.

These Words Sir Leoline first said,
When he rose and found his Lady dead:
These Words Sir Leoline will say
Many a Morn to his dying Day.

And hence the Custom and Law began,
That still at Dawn the Sacristan,
Who duly pulls the heavy Bell,
Five and forty Beads must tell
Between each Stroke – a warning Knell,
Which not a Soul can chuse but hear
From Bratha Head to Wyn'dermere.

Saith Bracy the Bard, 'So let it knell!
And let the drowsy Sacristan
Still count as slowly as he can!
There is no Lack of such, I ween,
As well fill up the Space between.
In Langdale Pike and Witch's Lair
And Dungeon-ghyll so foully rent,
With Ropes of Rock and Bells of Air
Three sinful Sextons' Ghosts are pent,
Who all give back, one after t'other,
The Death-note to their living Brother,
And oft too by the Knell offended,
Just as their One –! Two –! Three –! is ended,
The Devil mocks the doleful Tale
With a merry Peal from Borrowdale.'

The Air is still: thro' Mist and Cloud
That merry Peal comes ringing loud:
And Geraldine shakes off her dread
And rises lightly from the Bed;
Puts on her silken Vestments white,
And tricks her Hair in lovely Plight,
And nothing doubting of her Spell
Awakens the Lady Christabel.

'Sleep you, sweet Lady Christabel?
I trust, that you have rested well.'

And Christabel awoke and spied
The Same, who lay down by her Side –
O rather say, the Same whom She
Rais'd up beneath the old Oak Tree!
Nay, fairer yet! and yet more fair!
For She, belike, hath drunken deep
Of all the Blessedness of Sleep;
And while she spake; her Looks, her Air
Such gentle Thankfulness declare,
That (so it seem'd) her girded Vests
Grew tight beneath her heaving Breasts.
'Sure I have sinn'd!' said Christabel,
'Now Heaven be prais'd, if all be well!'
And in low faltering Tones, yet sweet
Did She the lofty Lady greet
With such Perplexity of Mind
As Dreams too lively leave behind.

So quickly she rose, and quickly array'd
Her maiden Limbs, and having pray'd
That He, who on the Cross did groan,
Might wash away her Sins unknown,
She forthwith led fair Geraldine
To meet her Sire, Sir Leoline.

The lovely Maid and the Lady tall
Are pacing both into the Hall,
And pacing on thro' Page and Groom
Enter the Baron's Presence Room.

The Baron rose and while he prest
His gentle Daughter to his Breast,
With chearful Wonder in his Eyes
The Lady Geraldine espies,

And gave such Welcome to the Same,
As might beseem so bright a Dame!

But when he heard the Lady's Tale
And when she told her Father's Name,
Why wax'd Sir Leoline so pale,
Murmuring o'er the Name again,
Lord Roland de Vaux of Tryermaine?
Alas! they had been Friends in Youth;
But whispering Tongues can poison Truth;
And Constancy lives in Realms above;
And Life is thorny; and Youth is vain;
And to be wroth with One, we love,
Doth work, like madness in the Brain:
And thus it chanc'd, as I divine,
With Roland and Sir Leoline.
Each spake words of high Disdain
And Insult to his Heart's best Brother:
They parted – ne'er to meet again!
But never either found Another
To free the hollow Heart from Paining –

They stood aloof, the scars remaining,
Like Cliffs, which had been rent asunder;
A dreary Sea now flows between,
But neither Heat, nor Frost, nor Thunder
Shall wholly do away, I ween,
The Marks of that, which once hath been.

Sir Leoline a moment's Space
Stood gazing on the Damsel's Face,
And the youthful Lord of Tryermaine
Came back upon his Heart again.

O then the Baron forgot his Age,
His noble Heart swell'd high with Rage;
He swore by the wounds in Jesu's Side,
He would proclaim it far and wide

With Trump and solemn Heraldry,
That they, who thus had wrong'd the Dame,
Were base as spotted Infamy!
'And if they dare deny the Same,
My Herald shall appoint a Week
And let the recreant Traitors seek
My Tournay Court – that there and then
I may dislodge their Reptile Souls
From the Bodies and Forms of Men!'
He spake: his eye in lightning rolls!
For the Lady was ruthlessly seiz'd; and he kenn'd
In the beautiful Lady the Child of his Friend!

And now the Tears were on his Face,
And fondly in his Arms he took
Fair Geraldine, who met th' Embrace
Prolonging it with Joyous Look.
Which when she view'd, a Vision fell
Upon the Soul of Christabel,
The Vision of Fear, the Touch and Pain!
She shrunk, and shudder'd, and saw again
(Ah woe is me! Was it for thee,
Thou gentle Maid! such Sights to see?)
Again she saw that Bosom old,
Again she felt that Bosom cold,
And drew in her Breath with a hissing Sound:
Whereat the Knight turn'd wildly round,
And nothing saw but his own sweet Maid
With Eyes uprais'd, as one that pray'd.

The Touch, the Sight, had pass'd away,
And in its Stead that Vision blest,
Which comforted her After rest,
While in the Lady's Arms she lay,
Had put a Rapture in her Breast,
And on her Lips and o'er her Eyes
Spread Smiles, like Light!

                          With new Surprize,
'What ails then my beloved Child?'
The Baron said – His Daughter mild
Made answer, 'All will yet be well!'
I ween, She had no Power to tell
Aught else: so mighty was the Spell.

Yet He, who saw this Geraldine,
Had deem'd her sure a Thing divine,
Such Sorrow with such Grace she blended,
As if she fear'd, she had offended
Sweet Christabel, that gentle Maid!
And with such lowly Tones she pray'd,
She might be sent without Delay
Home to her Father's Mansion.

                                'Nay!
Nay, by my Soul!' said Leoline.
'Ho! Bracy, the Bard, the Charge be thine!
Go thou with Music sweet and loud
And take two Steeds with Trappings proud
And take the Youth, whom thou lov'st best,
To bear thy Harp, and learn thy Song,
And cloath you both in solemn Vest,
And over the Mountains haste along,
Lest wandering Folk, that are abroad,
Detain you on the Valley Road.

'And when He has cross'd the Irthing Flood,
My merry Bard! He hastes, he hastes
Up Knorren Moor thro' Halegarth Wood,
And reaches soon that Castle good
Which stands and threatens Scotland's Wastes.

'Bard Bracy! Bard Bracy! Your Horses are fleet,
Ye must ride up the Hall, your Music so sweet
More loud than your Horses' echoing Feet!
And loud, and loud, to Lord Roland call,

Thy Daughter is safe in Langdale Hall!
Thy beautiful Daughter is safe and free –
Sir Leoline greets thee thus thro' me.
He bids thee come without Delay
With all thy numerous Array
And take thy lovely Daughter home,
And He will meet thee on the way
With all his numerous Array
White with their panting Palfrey's Foam;
And, by mine Honour! I will say,
That I repent me of the Day
When I spake words of fierce Disdain
To Roland de Vaux of Tryermaine! –
– For since that evil hour hath flown,
Many a Summer's Suns have shone;
Yet ne'er found I a Friend again
Like Roland de Vaux of Tryermaine.'

The Lady fell and clasp'd his Knees,
Her Face uprais'd, her Eyes o'erflowing;
And Bracy replied, with faltering Voice,
His gracious Hail on all bestowing.
'Thy Words, thou Sire of Christabel,
Are sweeter than my Harp can tell;
Yet might I gain a Boon of thee,
This Day my Journey should not be,
So strange a Dream hath come to me.
That I had vow'd with Music loud
To clear yon Wood from Thing unblest
Warn'd by a Vision in my Rest.

'For in my Sleep I saw that Dove,
That gentle Bird, whom thou dost love,
And call'st by thy own Daughter's Name,
Sir Leoline! I saw the Same
Fluttering and uttering fearful Moan
Among the green Herbs in the Forest alone.

Which when I saw and when I heard
I wonder'd what might ail the Bird:
For nothing near it could I see
Save the Grass and green Herbs underneath the old Tree.

'And in my Dream methought I went
To search out what might there be found,
And what the sweet Bird's Trouble meant
That thus lay fluttering on the Ground.
I went, and peer'd, and could descry
No cause for her distressful Cry;
But yet for her dear Lady's sake
I stoop'd, methought, the Dove to take,
When lo! I saw a bright green Snake
Coil'd around its Wings and Neck.
Green as the Herbs, on which it couch'd
Close by the Dove's its Head it crouch'd,
And with the Dove it heaves and stirs,
Swelling its Neck as she swell'd hers!

I woke; it was the Midnight Hour,
The Clock was echoing in the Tower;
But tho' my Slumber was gone by,
This Dream it would not pass away –
It seem'd to live upon my Eye!
And thence I vow'd this self-same Day
With Music strong and saintly Song
To wander thro' the Forest bare,
Lest aught unholy loiter there.'

Thus Bracy said: the Baron, the while,
Half-list'ning heard him with a Smile;
Then turn'd to Lady Geraldine,
His Eyes made up of Wonder and Love;
And said in courtly accents fine,
'Sweet Maid, Lord Roland's beauteous Dove,
With arms more strong than Harp or Song

Thy Sire and I will crush the Snake:'
He kiss'd her Forehead, as he spake,
And Geraldine in maiden wise
Casting down her large bright Eyes
With blushing Cheek and Courtesy fine
She turn'd her from Sir Leoline,
Softly gathering up her Train
That o'er her Right Arm fell again,
And folded her arms across her Chest,
And couch'd her Head upon her Breast;
And look'd askance at Christabel –
Jesu Maria, shield her well!

A Snake's small Eye blinks dull and shy;
And the Lady's Eyes they shrunk in her Head,
Each shrunk up to a Serpent's Eye,
And with somewhat of Malice and more of Dread
At Christabel she look'd askance! –
One moment – and the Sight was fled!
But Christabel in dizzy Trance
Stumbling on the unsteady Ground –
Shudder'd aloud with a hissing Sound;
And Geraldine again turn'd round,
And like a Thing, that sought Relief,
Full of Wonder and full of Grief,
She roll'd her large bright Eyes divine
Wildly on Sir Leoline.

The Maid, alas! her thoughts are gone
She nothing sees – no sight but one!
The Maid, devoid of Guile and Sin,
I know not how, in fearful wise
So deeply had she drunken in
That Look, those shrunken serpent Eyes,
That all her Features were resign'd
To this sole Image in her Mind:
And passively did imitate

That Look of dull and treacherous Hate.
And thus she stood in dizzy Trance
Still picturing that Look askance
With forc'd unconscious Sympathy
Full before her Father's View –
As far as such a Look could be
In Eyes so innocent and blue!

And when the Trance was o'er, the Maid
Paus'd awhile and inly pray'd,
Then falling at the Baron's Feet,
'By My Mother's Soul do I intreat
That Thou this Woman send away!'
She said; and more she could not say,
For what she knew, she could not tell
O'ermaster'd by the mighty Spell.

Why is thy Cheek so wan and wild,
Sir Leoline? – Thy only Child
Lies at thy Feet, thy Joy, thy Pride,
So fair, so innocent, so mild;
The same, for whom thy Lady died!
O by the Pangs of her dear Mother
Think thou no evil of thy Child!
For her and thee and for no other
She pray'd the moment, ere she died,
Pray'd, that the Babe for whom she died,
Might prove her dear Lord's Joy and Pride!
That Prayer her deadly Pangs beguil'd,
   Sir Leoline!
And would'st thou wrong thy only Child,
   Her Child and thine!

Within the Baron's Heart and Brain
If Thoughts, like these, had any Share,
They only swell'd his Rage and Pain
And did but work Confusion there.

His Heart was cleft with Pain and Rage,
His Cheeks they quiver'd, his Eyes were wild,
Dishonour'd thus in his old Age,
Dishonour'd by his only Child,
And all his Hospitality
To the wrong'd Daughter of his Friend
By more than woman's Jealousy
Brought thus to a disgraceful End –
He roll'd his Eye with stern Regard
Upon the gentle Minstrel Bard
And said in tones abrupt, austere –
'Why, Bracy! dost thou loiter here?
I bade thee hence!' The Bard obey'd;
And turning from his own sweet Maid
The aged Knight, Sir Leoline,
Led forth the Lady, Geraldine!

THE CONCLUSION TO PART II

A little Child, a limber Elf
Singing, dancing to itself;
A faery Thing with red round Cheeks,
That always *finds*, and never *seeks* –
Makes such a Vision to the Sight,
As fills a Father's Eyes with Light!
And Pleasures flow in so thick and fast
Upon his Heart, that he at last
Must needs express his Love's Excess
With Words of unmeant Bitterness.
Perhaps 'tis pretty to force together
Thoughts so all unlike each other;
To mutter and mock a broken Charm;
To dally with Wrong, that does no Harm –
Perhaps, 'tis tender too and pretty
At each wild Word to feel within
A sweet Recoil of Love and Pity.

And what if in a World of Sin
(O sorrow and shame! should this be true)
Such Giddiness of Heart and Brain
Comes seldom, save from Rage and Pain,
So talks, as it's most us'd to do.

[23] Frost at Midnight

The Frost performs its secret ministry,
Unhelped by any wind. The owlet's cry
Came loud – and hark, again! loud as before.
The inmates of my cottage, all at rest,
Have left me to that solitude, which suits
Abstruser musings: save that at my side
My cradled infant slumbers peacefully.
'Tis calm indeed! so calm, that it disturbs
And vexes meditation with its strange
And extreme silentness. Sea, hill, and wood,
This populous village! Sea, and hill, and wood,
With all the numberless goings on of life,
Inaudible as dreams! the thin blue flame
Lies on my low burnt fire, and quivers not;
Only that film, which fluttered on the grate,
Still flutters there, the sole unquiet thing.
Methinks, its motion in this hush of nature
Gives it dim sympathies with me who live,
Making it a companionable form,
Whose puny flaps and freaks the idling Spirit
By its own moods interprets, every where
Echo or mirror seeking of itself,
And makes a toy of Thought.

                         But O! how oft,
   How oft, at school, with most believing mind,
Presageful, have I gazed upon the bars,
To watch that fluttering *stranger!* and as oft
With unclosed lids, already had I dreamt
Of my sweet birth-place, and the old church-tower,
Whose bells, the poor man's only music, rang
From morn to evening, all the hot Fair-day,
So sweetly, that they stirred and haunted me

With a wild pleasure, falling on mine ear
Most like articulate sounds of things to come!
So gazed I, till the soothing things, I dreamt,
Lulled me to sleep, and sleep prolonged my dreams!
And so I brooded all the following morn,
Awed by the stern preceptor's face, mine eye
Fixed with mock study on my swimming book:
Save if the door half opened, and I snatched
A hasty glance, and still my heart leaped up,
For still I hoped to see the *stranger's* face,
Townsman, or aunt, or sister more beloved,
My play-mate when we both were clothed alike!

Dear Babe, that sleepest cradled by my side,
Whose gentle breathings, heard in this deep calm,
Fill up the interspersed vacancies
And momentary pauses of the thought!
My babe so beautiful! it thrills my heart
With tender gladness, thus to look at thee,
And think that thou shalt learn far other lore
And in far other scenes! For I was reared
In the great city, pent 'mid cloisters dim,
And saw nought lovely but the sky and stars.
But *thou*, my babe! shalt wander like a breeze
By lakes and sandy shores, beneath the crags
Of ancient mountain, and beneath the clouds,
Which image in their bulk both lakes and shores
And mountain crags: so shalt thou see and hear
The lovely shapes and sounds intelligible
Of that eternal language, which thy God
Utters, who from eternity doth teach
Himself in all, and all things in himself.
Great universal Teacher! he shall mould
Thy spirit, and by giving make it ask.

Therefore all seasons shall be sweet to thee,
Whether the summer clothe the general earth

With greenness, or the redbreast sit and sing
Betwixt the tufts of snow on the bare branch
Of mossy apple-tree, while the nigh thatch
Smokes in the sun-thaw; whether the eve-drops fall
Heard only in the trances of the blast,
Or if the secret ministry of frost
Shall hang them up in silent icicles,
Quietly shining to the quiet Moon.

[24] This Lime-tree Bower my Prison

ADVERTISEMENT
In the June of 1797, some long-expected Friends paid a visit to the Author's Cottage; and on the morning of their arrival, he met with an accident, which disabled him from walking during the whole time of their stay. One Evening, when they had left him for a few hours, he composed the following lines in the Garden-Bower.

Well, they are gone, and here must I remain,
This Lime-Tree Bower my Prison! I have lost
Beauties and Feelings, such as would have been
Most sweet to my remembrance, even when age
Had dimmed mine eyes to blindness! They, meanwhile,
Friends, whom I never more may meet again,
On springy heath, along the hill-top edge,
Wander in gladness, and wind down, perchance,
To that still roaring dell, of which I told;
The roaring dell, o'erwooded, narrow, deep,
And only speckled by the mid-day Sun;
Where its slim trunk the Ash from rock to rock
Flings arching like a Bridge; – that branchless Ash,
Unsunn'd and damp, whose few poor yellow leaves
Ne'er tremble in the gale, yet tremble still,
Fann'd by the water-fall! and there my friends
Behold the dark green file of long* lank Weeds,
That all at once (a most fantastic sight!)
Still nod and drip beneath the dripping edge
Of the blue clay-stone.

                         Now, my Friends emerge
Beneath the wide wide Heaven – and view again
The many-steepled track magnificent
Of hilly fields and meadows, and the sea,
With some fair bark, perhaps, whose Sails light up
The slip of smooth clear blue betwixt two Isles

Of purple shadow! Yes! they wander on
In gladness all; but thou, methinks, most glad,
My gentle-hearted Charles! for thou hast pined
And hunger'd after Nature, many a year,
In the great City pent, winning thy way
With sad yet patient soul, through evil and pain
And strange calamity! Ah! slowly sink
Behind the western ridge, thou glorious Sun!
Shine in the slant beams of the sinking orb
Ye purple heath-flowers! richlier burn, ye clouds!
Live in the yellow light, ye distant groves!
And kindle, thou blue Ocean! So my Friend
Struck with deep joy may stand, as I have stood,
Silent with swimming sense; yea, gazing round
On the wide landscape, gaze till all doth seem
Less gross than bodily: and of such hues
As veil the Almighty Spirit, when he makes
Spirits perceive his presence.

                              A delight
Comes sudden on my heart, and I am glad
As I myself were there! Nor in this bower,
This little lime-tree bower, have I not mark'd
Much that has sooth'd me. Pale beneath the blaze
Hung the transparent foliage; and I watch'd
Some broad and sunny leaf, and lov'd to see
The shadow of the leaf and stem above
Dappling its sunshine! And that Walnut-tree
Was richly ting'd, and a deep radiance lay
Full on the ancient Ivy, which usurps
Those fronting elms, and now, with blackest mass
Makes their dark branches gleam a lighter hue
Through the late twilight: and though now the Bat
Wheels silent by, and not a Swallow twitters,
Yet still the solitary humble Bee
Sings in the bean-flower! Henceforth I shall know

That Nature ne'er deserts the wise and pure,
No Plot so narrow, be but Nature there,
No waste so vacant, but may well employ
Each faculty of sense, and keep the heart
Awake to Love and Beauty! and sometimes
'Tis well to be bereft of promised good,
That we may lift the Soul, and contemplate
With lively joy the joys we cannot share.
My gentle-hearted Charles! when the last Rook
Beat its straight path along the dusky air
Homewards, I blest it! deeming, its black wing
(Now a dim speck, now vanishing in light)
Had cross'd the mighty Orb's dilated glory,
While thou stood'st gazing; or when all was still,
Flew creeking o'er thy head, and had a charm
For thee, my gentle-hearted Charles, to whom
No Sound is dissonant which tells of Life.

* *Of long lank Weeds.* The Asplenium Scolopendrium, called in some
countries the Adder's Tongue, in others the Hart's Tongue: but Withering
gives the Adder's Tongue as the trivial name of Ophioglossum only.

[25] The Mad Monk

I heard a voice from Etna's side;
  Where, o'er a cavern's mouth
  That fronted to the south,
A chestnut spread its umbrage wide:
A hermit, or a monk, the man might be;
But him I could not see;
And thus the music flow'd along,
In melody most like to old Sicilian song:

'There was a time when earth, and sea, and skies,
  The bright green vale, and forest's dark recess,
With all things, lay before mine eyes
  In steady loveliness:
But now I feel, on earth's uneasy scene,
  Such sorrows as will never cease; –
  I only ask for peace;
If I must live to know that such a time has been!'
A silence then ensued:

  Till from the cavern came
  A voice; – it was the same!
And thus, in mournful tone, its dreary plaint renew'd:

'Last night, as o'er the sloping turf I trod,
  The smooth green turf, to me a vision gave
Beneath mine eyes, the sod –
  The roof of ROSA's grave!
My heart has need with dreams like these to strive;
  For, when I woke, beneath mine eyes, I found
  The plot of mossy ground,
On which we oft have sat when ROSA was alive. –
Why must the rock, and margin of the flood,
  Why must the hills so many flow'ret's bear,
  Whose colours to a *murder'd* maiden's blood

Such sad resemblance wear? –
I struck the wound, – this hand of mine!
For Oh, thou maid divine,
   I lov'd to agony!
The youth whom thou call'dst thine
   Did never love like me?

'Is it the stormy clouds above
   That flash'd so red a gleam?
   On yonder downward trickling stream? –
'Tis not the blood of her I love. –
The sun torments me from his western bed,
   Oh, let him cease for ever to diffuse
   Those crimson spectre hues!
Oh, let me lie in peace, and be for ever dead!'

Here ceas'd the voice. In deep dismay,
Down thro' the forest I pursu'd my way.

[26] A Letter to –

Well! if the Bard was weatherwise, who made
The grand old Ballad of Sir Patrick Spence,
This Night, so tranquil now, will not go hence
Unrous'd by winds, that ply a busier trade
Than that, which moulds yon clouds in lazy flakes,
Or the dull sobbing Draft, that drones & rakes
Upon the Strings of this Eolian Lute,
    Which better far were mute.
For, lo! the New Moon, winter-bright!
And overspread with phantom Light,
(With swimming phantom Light o'erspread
But rimm'd & circled with a silver Thread)
I see the Old Moon in her Lap, foretelling
The coming-on of Rain & squally Blast –
O! Sara! that the Gust ev'n now were swelling,
And the slant Night-shower driving loud & fast!

A Grief without a pang, void, dark, & drear,
A stifling, drowsy, unimpassion'd Grief
That finds no natural Outlet, no Relief
    In word, or sigh, or tear –
This, Sara! well thou know'st,
Is that sore Evil, which I dread the Most,
And oft'nest suffer! In this heartless Mood
To other thoughts by yonder Throstle woo'd,
That pipes within the Larch-tree, not unseen,
(The Larch, which pushes out in tassels green
It's bundled Leafits) woo'd to mild Delights
By all the tender Sounds & gentle Sights
Of this sweet Primrose-month – & *vainly* woo'd
O dearest Sara! in this heartless Mood
All this long Eve, so balmy & serene,
Have I been gazing on the western Sky

And it's peculiar Tint of Yellow Green –
And still I gaze – & with how blank an eye!
And those thin Clouds above, in flakes & bars,
That give away their Motion to the Stars;
Those Stars, that glide behind them, or between,
Now sparkling, now bedimm'd, but always seen;
Yon crescent Moon, as fix'd as if it grew
In it's own cloudless, starless Lake of Blue –
A boat becalm'd dear William's Sky Canoe!
– I see them all, so excellently fair!
  I see, not feel, how beautiful they are.

    My genial Spirits fail –
    And what can these avail
To lift the smoth'ring Weight from off my Breast?
    It were a vain Endeavor,
    Tho' I should gaze for ever
On that Green Light which lingers in the West!
I may not hope from outward Forms to win
The Passion & the Life whose Fountains are within!
These lifeless Shapes, around, below, Above,
    O what can they impart?
When even the gentle Thought, that thou, my Love!
    Art gazing now, like me,
    And see'st the Heaven, I see –
Sweet Thought it is – yet feebly stirs my Heart!

    Feebly! O feebly! – Yet
    (I well remember it)
In my first Dawn of Youth that Fancy stole
With many secret Yearnings on my Soul.
At eve, sky-gazing in 'ecstatic fit'
(Alas! for cloister'd in a city School
The Sky was all, I knew, of Beautiful)
At the barr'd window often did I sit,
And oft upon the leaded School-roof lay,
  And to myself would say –

There does not live the Man so stripp'd of good affections
As not to love to see a Maiden's quiet Eyes
Uprais'd, and linking on sweet Dreams by dim Connections
To Moon, or Evening Star, or glorious western Skies –
While yet a Boy, this Thought would so pursue me
That often it became a kind of Vision to me!

    Sweet Thought! and dear of old
    To Hearts of finer Mould!
Ten thousand times by Friends & Lovers blest!
    I spake with rash Despair,
    And ere I was aware,
The Weight was somewhat lifted from my Breast!
O Sara! in the weather-fended Wood,
Thy lov'd haunt! where the Stock-doves coo at Noon,
    I guess, that thou has stood
And watch'd yon Crescent, & it's ghost-like Moon.
And yet, far rather in my present Mood
I would, that thou'dst been sitting all this while
Upon the sod-built Seat of Camomile –
And tho' thy Robin may have ceas'd to sing,
Yet needs for *my* sake must thou love to hear
The Bee-hive murmuring near,
That ever-busy & most quiet Thing
Which I have heard at Midnight murmuring.

    I feel my spirit moved –
    And wheresoe'er thou be,
    O Sister! O Beloved!
    Those dear mild Eyes, that see
    Even now the Heaven, *I* see –
There is a Prayer in them! It is for *me* –
And I, dear Sara – *I* am blessing *thee*!

It was as calm as this, that happy night
When Mary, thou, & I together were,
The low decaying Fire our only Light,

And listen'd to the Stillness of the Air!
O that affectionate & blameless Maid,
Dear Mary! on her Lap my head she lay'd –
     Her Hand was on my Brow,
     Even as my own is now;
And on my Cheek I felt thy eye-lash play.
Such Joy I had, that I may truly say,
My Spirit was awe-stricken with the Excess
And trance-like Depth of it's brief Happiness.

Ah fair Remembrances, that so revive
The Heart, & fill it with a living Power,
Where were they, Sara? – or did I not strive
To win them to me? – on the fretting Hour
Then when I wrote thee that complaining Scroll
Which even to bodily Sickness bruis'd thy Soul!
And yet thou blam'st thyself alone! And yet
     Forbidd'st me all Regret!

And must I not regret, that I distress'd
Thee, best belov'd! who lovest me the best?
My better mind had fled, I know not whither,
For o! was this an Absent Friend's Employ
To send from far both Pain & Sorrow thither
Where still his Blessings should have call'd down Joy!
I read thy guileless Letter o'er again –
I hear thee of thy blameless Self complain –
And only this I learn – & this, alas! I know –
That thou art weak & pale with Sickness, Grief, & Pain –
     And *I – I* made thee so!

O for my own sake I regret perforce
Whatever turns thee, Sara! from the Course
Of calm Well-being & a Heart at rest!
When thou, & with thee those, whom thou lov'st best,
Shall dwell together in one happy Home,
One House, the dear *abiding* Home of All,

I too will crown me with a Coronal —
Nor shall this Heart in idle Wishes roam
    Morbidly soft!
No! let me trust, that I shall wear away
In no inglorious Toils the manly Day,
And only now & then, & not too oft,
Some dear & memorable Eve will bless
Dreaming of all your Loves & Quietness.

Be happy, & I need thee not in sight.
Peace in thy Heart, & Quiet in thy Dwelling,
Health in thy Limbs, & in thine Eyes the Light
Of Love, & Hope, & honorable Feeling —
Where e'er I am, I shall be well content!
Not near thee, haply shall be more content!
To all things I prefer the Permanent.
And better seems it for a heart, like mine,
Always to *know*, than sometimes to behold,
    Their Happiness & thine —
For Change doth trouble me with pangs untold!
To see thee, hear thee, feel thee — then to part
    Oh! — it weighs down the Heart!
To *visit* those, I love, as I love thee,
Mary, & William, & dear Dorothy,
It is but a temptation to repine —
The transientness is Poison in the Wine,
Eats out the pith of Joy, makes all Joy hollow,
All Pleasure a dim Dream of Pain to follow!
My own peculiar Lot, my house-hold Life
It is, & will remain, Indifference or Strife —
While *ye* are *well & happy*, twould but wrong you —
If I should fondly yearn to be among you —
Wherefore, O wherefore! should I wish to be
A wither'd branch upon a blossoming Tree?

But (let me say it! for I vainly strive
To beat away the Thought) but if thou pin'd,

Whate'er the Cause, in body, or in mind,
I were the miserablest Man alive
To know it & be absent! Thy Delights
Far off, or near, alike I may partake –
But o! to mourn for thee, & to forsake
All power, all hope of giving comfort to thee –
To know that thou are weak & and worn with pain,
And not to hear thee, Sara! not to view thee –

 Not sit beside thy Bed,
 Not press thy aching Head,
 Not bring thee Health again –
 At least to hope, to try –
By this Voice, which thou lov'st, & by this earnest Eye –
Nay, wherefore did I let it haunt my Mind
 The dark distressful Dream!
I turn from it, & listen to the Wind
Which long has rav'd unnotic'd! What a Scream
Of agony by Torture lengthen'd out
That Lute sent forth! O thou wild Storm without!
Jagg'd Rock, or mountain Pond, or blasted Tree,
Or Pine-grove, Whither Woodman never clomb,
Or lonely House, long held the Witches' Home,
Methinks were fitter Instruments for Thee,
Mad Lutanist! that in this month of Showers,
Of dark brown Gardens, & of peeping Flowers,
Mak'st Devil's Yule, with worse than wintry Song
The Blossoms, Buds, and timorous Leaves among!
Thou Actor, perfect in all tragic Sounds!
Thou mighty Poet, even to frenzy bold!
 What tell'st thou now about?
'Tis of the Rushing of an Host in Rout –
And many Groans from men with smarting Wounds –
At once they groan with smart, and shudder with the Cold!
Tis hush'd! there is a Trance of deepest Silence,
Again! but all that Sound, as of a rushing Crowd,
And Groans & tremulous Shudderings, all are over –

And it has other Sounds, and all less deep, less loud!
A Tale of less Affright,
And temper'd with Delight,
As William's Self had made the tender Lay –
Tis of a little Child
Upon a heathy Wild,
Not far from home – but it has lost it's way –
And now moans low in utter grief & fear –
And now screams loud, & hopes to make it's Mother hear!

Tis Midnight! and small Thoughts have I of Sleep –
Full seldom may my Friend such Vigils keep –
O breathe She softly in her gentle Sleep!
Cover her, gentle Sleep! with wings of Healing –
And be this Tempest but a Mountain Birth!
May all the Stars hang bright above her Dwelling,
Silent, as tho' they *watch'd* the sleeping Earth!
Healthful & light, my Darling! may'st thou rise
With clear & chearful Eyes –
And of the same good Tidings to me send!
For, oh! beloved Friend!
I am not the buoyant Thing, I was of yore –
When like an own Child, I to Joy belong'd;
For others mourning oft, myself oft sorely wrong'd,
Yet bearing all things then, as if I nothing bore!

Yes, dearest Sara! Yes!
There *was* a time when tho' my path was rough,
The Joy within me dallied with Distress;
And all Misfortunes were but as the Stuff
Whence Fancy made me Dreams of Happiness:
For Hope grew round me, like the climbing Vine,
And Leaves & Fruitage, not my own, seem'd mine!
But now Ill Tidings bow me down to earth/
Nor care I, that they rob me of my Mirth/
But oh! each Visitation
Suspends what Nature gave me at my Birth,

My shaping Spirit of Imagination!
I speak not now of those habitual Ills
That wear out Life, when two unequal Minds
Meet in one House, & two discordant Wills –
    This leaves me, where it finds,
Past cure, & past Complaint – a fate Austere
Too fix'd & hopeless to partake of Fear!

But thou, dear Sara! (dear indeed thou art,
My Comforter! A Heart within my Heart!)
Thou, & the Few, we love, tho' few ye be,
Make up a world of Hopes & Fears for me.
And if Affliction, or distemp'ring Pain,
Or wayward Chance befall you, I complain
Not that I mourn – O Friends, most dear! most true!
    Methinks to weep with you
Were better far than to rejoice alone –
But that my coarse domestic Life has known
No Habits of heart-nursing Sympathy,
No Griefs, but such as dull and deaden me,
No mutual mild Enjoyments of it's own,
No Hopes of it's own Vintage, None, o! none –
Whence when I mourn'd for you, my Heart might borrow
Fair forms & living Motions for it's Sorrow.
For not to think of what I needs must feel,
But to be still & patient all I can;
And haply by abstruse Research to steal
From my own Nature all the Natural Man –
This was my sole Resource, my wisest plan!
And that, which suits a part, infects the whole,
And now is almost grown the Temper of my Soul.

My little Children are a Joy, a Love,
    A good Gift from above!
But what is Bliss, that still calls up a Woe,
    And makes it doubly keen
Compelling me to *feel*, as well as Know,

What a most blessed Lot mine might have been.
Those little Angel Children (woe is me!)
There have been hours, when feeling how they bind
And pluck out the Wing-feathers of my Mind,
Turning my Error to Necessity,
I have half-wish'd, they never had been born!
That seldom! But sad Thoughts they always bring,
And like the Poet's Philomel, I sing
My Love-song, with my breast against a Thorn.

With no unthankful Spirit I confess,
This clinging Grief too, in it's turn, awakes
That Love, and Father's Joy; but O! it makes
The Love the greater, & the Joy far less,
These Mountains too, these Vales, these Woods, these Lakes,
Scenes full of Beauty & of Loftiness
Where all my Life I fondly hop'd to live –
I were sunk low indeed, did they *no* solace give;
But oft I seem to feel, & evermore I fear,
They are not to me now the Things, which once they were.

O Sara! we receive but what we give,
And in *our* Life alone does Nature live.
Our's is her Wedding Garment, our's her Shroud –
And would we aught behold of higher Worth
Than that inanimate cold World allow'd
To the poor loveless ever-anxious Crowd,
Ah! from the Soul itself must issue forth
A Light, a Glory, and a luminous Cloud
        Enveloping the Earth!
And from the Soul itself must there be sent
A sweet & potent Voice, of it's own Birth,
Of all sweet Sounds the Life & Element.

O pure of Heart! thou need'st not ask of me
What this strong music in the Soul may be,
        What, & wherein it doth exist,

This Light, this Glory, this fair luminous Mist,
This beautiful & beauty-making Power!
Joy, innocent Sara! Joy, that ne'er was given
Save to the Pure, & in their purest Hour,
Joy, Sara! is the Spirit & the Power,
That wedding Nature to us gives in Dower
    A new Earth & new Heaven
Undreamt of by the Sensual & the Proud!
Joy is that strong Voice, Joy that luminous Cloud –
    We, we ourselves rejoice!
And thence flows all that charms or ear or sight,
All melodies the Echoes of that Voice,
All Colors a Suffusion of that Light.

Sister & Friend of my devoutest Choice!
Thou being innocent & full of love,
And nested with the Darlings of thy Love,
And feeling in thy Soul, Heart, Lips, & Arms
Even what the conjugal & mother Dove
That borrows genial Warmth from those, she warms,
Feels in her thrill'd wings, blessedly outspread –
Thou free'd awhile from Cares & human Dread
By the Immenseness of the Good & Fair
    Which thou see'st every where –
Thus, thus should'st thou rejoice!
To thee would all Things live from Pole to Pole,
Their Life the Eddying of thy living Soul.
O dear! O Innocent! O full of Love!
A very Friend! A Sister of my Choice –
O dear, as Light & Impulse from above,
Thus may'st thou ever, evermore rejoice!

[27] Dejection: An Ode

Late, late yestreen I saw the new Moon,
With the old Moon in her arms;
And I fear, I fear, my Master dear!
We shall have a deadly storm.
                    Ballad of Sir PATRICK SPENCE.

I

Well! If the Bard was weather-wise, who made
  The grand old ballad of Sir Patrick Spence,
  This night, so tranquil now, will not go hence
Unrous'd by winds, that ply a busier trade
Than those which mould yon clouds in lazy flakes,
Or the dull sobbing draft, that moans and rakes
    Upon the strings of this Æolian lute,
    Which better far were mute.
  For lo! the New-moon winter-bright!
  And overspread with phantom-light,
  (With swimming phantom-light o'erspread
  But rimm'd and circled by a silver thread)
I see the old Moon in her lap, foretelling
  The coming on of rain and squally blast.
And oh! that even now the gust were swelling,
  And the slant night-shower driving loud and fast!
Those sounds which oft have raised me, whilst they awed,
    And sent my soul abroad,
Might now perhaps their wonted impulse give,
Might startle this dull pain, and make it move and live!

II

A grief without a pang, void, dark, and drear,
  A stifled, drowsy, unimpassion'd grief,
  Which finds no natural outlet, no relief,

In word, or sigh, or tear –
O Lady! in this wan and heartless mood,
To other thoughts by yonder throstle woo'd,
    All this long eve, so balmy and serene,
Have I been gazing on the western sky,
    And it's peculiar tint of yellow green:
And still I gaze – and with how blank an eye!
And those thin clouds above, in flakes and bars,
That give away their motion to the stars;
Those stars, that glide behind them or between,
Now sparkling, now bedimm'd, but always seen;
Yon crescent Moon, as fix'd as if it grew
In its own cloudless, starless lake of blue;
I see them all so excellently fair,
I see, not feel how beautiful they are!

III

    My genial spirits fail,
    And what can these avail,
To lift the smoth'ring weight from off my breast?
    It were a vain endeavor,
    Though I should gaze for ever
On that green light that lingers in the west:
I may not hope from outward forms to win
The passion and the life, whose fountains are within.

IV

O Lady! we receive but what we give,
And in our life alone does nature live:
Ours is her wedding-garment, ours her shroud!
    And would we aught behold, of higher worth,
Than that inanimate cold world allow'd
To the poor loveless ever-anxious crowd,
    Ah! from the soul itself must issue forth,
A light, a glory, a fair luminous cloud

Enveloping the Earth –
And from the soul itself must there be sent
    A sweet and potent voice, of its own birth,
Of all sweet sounds the life and element!

V

O pure of heart! thou need'st not ask of me
What this strong music in the soul may be!
What, and wherein it doth exist,
This light, this glory, this fair luminous mist,
This beautiful, and beauty-making power.
    Joy, virtuous Lady! Joy that ne'er was given,
Save to the pure, and in their purest hour.
Life, and Life's Effluence, Cloud at once and Shower,
Joy, Lady! is the spirit and the power,
Which wedding Nature to us gives in dow'r
    A new Earth and new Heaven,
Undreamt of by the sensual and the proud –
Joy is the sweet voice, Joy the luminous cloud –
        We in ourselves rejoice!
And thence flows all that charms or ear or sight,
    All melodies the echoes of that voice,
All colours a suffusion from that light.

VI

There was a time when, though my path was rough,
    This joy within me dallied with distress,
And all misfortunes were but as the stuff
    Whence Fancy made me dreams of happiness:
For hope grew round me, like the twining vine,
And fruits, and foliage, not my own, seem'd mine.
But now afflictions bow me down to earth:
Nor care I that they rob me of my mirth,
        But oh! each visitation
Suspends what nature gave me at my birth,

My shaping spirit of Imagination.
For not to think of what I needs must feel,
   But to be still and patient, all I can;
And haply by abstruse research to steal
   From my own nature all the natural Man –
   This was my sole resource, my only plan:
Till that which suits a part infects the whole,
And now is almost grown the habit of my Soul.

VII

Hence, viper thoughts, that coil around my mind,
   Reality's dark dream!
I turn from you, and listen to the wind,
   Which long has rav'd unnotic'd. What a scream
Of agony by torture lengthen'd out
That lute sent forth! Thou Wind, that rav'st without,
   Bare crag, or mountain-tairn,* blasted tree,
Or pine-grove whither woodman never clomb,
Or lonely house, long held the witches' home,
   Methinks were fitter instruments for thee,
Mad Lutanist! who in this month of show'rs,
Of dark brown gardens, and of peeping flow'rs,
Mak'st Devils' yule, with worse than wint'ry song,
The blossoms, buds, and tim'rous leaves among.
   Thou Actor, perfect in all tragic sounds!
Thou mighty Poet, e'en to Frenzy bold!
      What tell'st thou now about?
      'Tis of the Rushing of an Host in rout,
   With groans of trampled men, with smarting wounds –
At once they groan with pain, and shudder with the cold!
But hush! there is a pause of deepest silence!
   And all that noise, as of a rushing crowd,
With groans, and tremulous shudderings – all is over –
   It tells another tale, with sounds less deep and loud!
      A tale of less affright,

And temper'd with delight,
As Otway's self had fram'd the tender lay –
　　'Tis of a little child
　　Upon a lonesome wild,
Not far from home, but she hath lost her way:
And now moans low in bitter grief and fear,
And now screams loud, and hopes to make her mother hear.

VIII

'Tis midnight, but small thoughts have I of sleep:
Full seldom may my friend such vigils keep!
Visit her, gentle Sleep! with wings of healing,
　　And may this storm be but a mountain-birth,
May all the stars hang bright above her dwelling,
　　Silent as though they watch'd the sleeping Earth!
　　　With light heart may she rise,
　　　　Gay fancy, cheerful eyes,
　　Joy lift her spirit, joy attune her voice:
To her may all things live, from Pole to Pole,
Their life the eddying of her living soul!
　　O simple spirit, guided from above,
Dear Lady! friend devoutest of my choice,
Thus may'st thou ever, evermore rejoice.

* Tairn is a small lake, generally if not always applied to the lakes up in
the mountains, and which are the feeders of those in the vallies. This
address to the Storm-wind will not appear extravagant to those who have
heard it at night, and in a mountainous country.

[28] The Ancyent Marinere (1798)

ARGUMENT

How a Ship having passed the Line was driven by Storms to the cold Country towards the South Pole; and how from thence she made her course to the tropical Latitude of the Great Pacific Ocean; and of the strange things that befell; and in what manner the Ancyent Marinere came back to his own Country.

I

It is an ancyent Marinere,
   And he stoppeth one of three:
'By thy long grey beard and thy glittering eye
   'Now wherefore stoppest me?

'The Bridegroom's doors are open'd wide
   'And I am next of kin;
'The Guests are met, the Feast is set, –
   'May'st hear the merry din.

But still he holds the wedding-guest –
   There was a Ship, quoth he –
'Nay, if thou'st got a laughsome tale,
   'Marinere! come with me.'

He holds him with his skinny hand,
   Quoth he, there was a Ship –
'Now get thee hence, thou grey-beard Loon!
   'Or my Staff shall make thee skip.

He holds him with his glittering eye –
   The wedding guest stood still
And listens like a three year's child;
   The Marinere hath his will.

The wedding-guest sate on a stone,
   He cannot chuse but hear:

And thus spake on that ancyent man,
  The bright-eyed Marinere.

The Ship was cheer'd, the Harbour clear'd –
  Merrily did we drop
Below the Kirk, below the Hill,
  Below the Light-house top.

The Sun came up upon the left,
  Out of the Sea came he:
And he shone bright, and on the right
  Went down into the Sea.

Higher and higher every day,
  Till over the mast at noon –
The wedding-guest here beat his breast,
  For he heard the loud bassoon.

The Bride hath pac'd into the Hall,
  Red as a rose is she;
Nodding their heads before her goes
  The merry Minstralsy.

The wedding-guest he beat his breast,
  Yet he cannot chuse but hear:
And thus spake on that ancyent Man,
  The bright-eyed Marinere.

Listen, Stranger! Storm and Wind,
  A Wind and Tempest strong!
For days and weeks it play'd us freaks –
  Like Chaff we drove along.

Listen, Stranger! Mist and Snow,
  And it grew wond'rous cauld:
And Ice mast-high came floating by
  As green as Emerauld.

And thro' the drifts the snowy clifts
  Did send a dismal sheen;

Ne shapes of men ne beasts we ken –
    The Ice was all between.

The Ice was here, the Ice was there,
    The Ice was all around:
It crack'd and growl'd, and roar'd and howl'd –
    Like noises of a swound.

At length did cross an Albatross,
    Thorough the Fog it came;
And an it were a Christian Soul,
    We hail'd it in God's name.

The Marineres gave it biscuit-worms,
    And round and round it flew:
The Ice did split with a Thunder-fit;
    The Helmsman steer'd us thro'.

And a good south wind sprung up behind,
    The Albatross did follow;
And every day for food or play
    Came to the Marinere's hollo!

In mist or cloud on mast or shroud
    It perch'd for vespers nine,
Whiles all the night thro' fog-smoke white
    Glimmer'd the white moon-shine.

'God save thee, ancyent Marinere!
    'From the fiends that plague thee thus –
'Why look'st thou so?' – with my cross bow
    I shot the Albatross.

II

The Sun came up upon the right,
    Out of the Sea came he;
And broad as a weft upon the left
    Went down into the Sea.

And the good south wind still blew behind,
   But no sweet Bird did follow
Ne any day for food or play
   Came to the Marinere's hollo!

And I had done an hellish thing
   And it would work 'em woe:
For all averr'd, I had kill'd the Bird
   That made the Breeze to blow.

Ne dim ne red, like God's own head,
   The glorious Sun uprist:
Then all averr'd, I had kill'd the Bird
   That brought the fog and mist.
'Twas right, said they, such birds to slay
   That bring the fog and mist.

The breezes blew, the white foam flew,
   The furrow follow'd free:
We were the first that ever burst
   Into that silent Sea.

Down dropt the breeze, the Sails dropt down,
   'Twas sad as sad could be
And we did speak only to break
   The silence of the Sea.

All in a hot and copper sky
   The bloody sun at noon,
Right up above the mast did stand,
   No bigger than the moon.

Day after day, day after day,
   We stuck, ne breath ne motion,
As idle as a painted Ship
   Upon a painted Ocean.

Water, water, every where
   And all the boards did shrink;

Water, water, every where,
    Ne any drop to drink.

The very deeps did rot: O Christ!
    That ever this should be!
Yea, slimy things did crawl with legs
    Upon the slimy Sea.

About, about, in reel and rout
    The Death-fires danc'd at night;
The water, like a witch's oils,
    Burnt green and blue and white.

And some in dreams assured were
    Of the Spirit that plagued us so:
Nine fathom deep he had follow'd us
    From the Land of Mist and Snow.

And every tongue thro' utter drouth
    Was wither'd at the root;
We could not speak no more than if
    We had been choked with soot.

Ah wel-a-day! what evil looks
    Had I from old and young;
Instead of the Cross the Albatross
    About my neck was hung.

III

I saw a something in the Sky
    No bigger than my fist;
At first it seem'd a little speck
    And then it seem'd a mist:
It mov'd and mov'd, and took at last
    A certain shape, I wist.

A speck, a mist, a shape, I wist!
    And still it ner'd and ner'd;

And, an it dodg'd a water-sprite,
  It plung'd and tack'd and veer'd.

With throat unslack'd, with black lips bak'd
  Ne could we laugh, ne wail:
Then while thro' drouth all dumb they stood
I bit my arm and suck'd the blood
  And cry'd, A sail! a sail!

With throat unslack'd, with black lips bak'd
  Agape they hear'd me call:
Gramercy! they for joy did grin
And all at once their breath drew in
  As they were drinking all.

She doth not tack from side to side –
  Hither to work us weal
Withouten wind, withouten tide
  She steddies with upright keel.

The western wave was all a flame,
  The day was well nigh done!
Almost upon the western wave
  Rested the broad bright Sun;
When that strange shape drove suddenly
  Betwixt us and the Sun.

And strait the Sun was fleck'd with bars
  (Heaven's mother send us grace)
As if thro' a dungeon grate he peer'd
  With broad and burning face.

Alas! (thought I, and my heart beat loud)
  How fast she neres and neres!
Are those *her* Sails that glance in the Sun
  Like restless gossameres?

Are these *her* naked ribs, which fleck'd
  The sun that did behind them peer?

And are these two all, all the crew,
    That woman and her fleshless Pheere?

His bones were black with many a crack,
    All black and bare, I ween;
Jet-black and bare, save where with rust
Of mouldy damps and charnel crust
    They're patch'd with purple and green.

Her lips are red, *her* looks are free,
    Her locks are yellow as gold:
Her skin is as white as leprosy,
And she is far liker Death than he;
    Her flesh makes the still air cold.

The naked Hulk alongside came
    And the Twain were playing dice;
'The Game is done! I've won, I've won!'
    Quoth she, and whistled thrice.

A gust of wind sterte up behind
    And whistled thro' his bones;
Thro' the holes of his eyes and the hole of his mouth
    Half-whistles and half-groans.

With never a whisper in the Sea
    Off darts the Spectre-ship;
While clombe above the Eastern bar
The horned Moon, the one bright Star
    Almost atween the tips.

One after one by the horned Moon
    (Listen, O Stranger! to me)
Each turn'd his face with a ghastly pang
    And curs'd me with his ee.

Four times fifty living men,
    With never a sigh or groan,

With heavy thump, a lifeless lump
    They dropp'd down one by one.

Their souls did from their bodies fly, –
    They fled to bliss or woe;
And every soul it pass'd me by,
    Like the whiz of my Cross-bow.

IV

'I fear thee, ancyent Marinere!
    'I fear thy skinny hand;
'And thou art long and lank and brown
    'As is the ribb'd Sea-sand.

'I fear thee and thy glittering eye
    'And thy skinny hand so brown –
Fear not, fear not, thou wedding guest!
    This body dropt not down.

Alone, alone, all all alone
    Alone on the wide wide Sea;
And Christ would take no pity on
    My soul in agony.

The many men so beautiful,
    And they all dead did lie!
And a million million slimy things
    Liv'd on – and so did I.

I look'd upon the rotting Sea,
    And drew my eyes away;
I look'd upon the eldritch deck,
    And there the dead men lay.

I look'd to Heaven, and try'd to pray;
    But or ever a prayer had gusht,
A wicked whisper came and made
    My heart as dry as dust.

I clos'd my lids and kept them close,
    Till the balls like pulses beat;
For the sky and the sea, and the sea and the sky
Lay like a load on my weary eye,
    And the dead were at my feet.

The cold sweat melted from their limbs,
    Ne rot, ne reek did they;
The look with which they look'd on me,
    Had never pass'd away.

An orphan's curse would drag to Hell
    A spirit from on high:
But O! more horrible than that
    Is the curse in a dead man's eye!
Seven days, seven nights I saw that curse,
    And yet I could not die.

The moving Moon went up the sky
    And no where did abide:
Softly she was going up
    And a star or two beside –

Her beams bemock'd the sultry main
    Like morning frosts yspread;
But where the ship's huge shadow lay,
The charmed water burnt alway
    A still and awful red.

Beyond the shadow of the ship
    I watch'd the water-snakes:
They mov'd in tracks of shining white;
And when they rear'd, the elfish light
    Fell off in hoary flakes.

Within the shadow of the ship
    I watch'd their rich attire:
Blue, glossy green, and velvet black

They coil'd and swam; and every track
  Was a flash of golden fire.

O happy living things! no tongue
  Their beauty might declare:
A spring of love gusht from my heart,
  And I bless'd them unaware!
Sure my kind saint took pity on me,
  And I bless'd them unaware.

The self-same moment I could pray;
  And from my neck so free
The Albatross fell off, and sank
  Like lead into the sea.

v

O sleep, it is a gentle thing
  Belov'd from pole to pole!
To Mary-queen the praise be yeven
She sent the gentle sleep from heaven
  That slid into my soul.

The silly buckets on the deck
  That had so long remain'd,
I dreamt that they were fill'd with dew
  And when I awoke it rain'd.

My lips were wet, my throat was cold,
  My garments all were dank;
Sure I had drunken in my dreams
  And still my body drank.

I mov'd and could not feel my limbs,
  I was so light, almost
I thought that I had died in sleep,
  And was a blessed Ghost.

The roaring wind! it roar'd far off,
    It did not come anear;
But with its sound it shook the sails
    That were so thin and sere.

The upper air bursts into life,
    And a hundred fire-flags sheen
To and fro they are hurried about;
And to and fro, and in and out
    The stars dance on between.

The coming wind doth roar more loud;
    The sails do sigh, like sedge:
The rain pours down from one black cloud
    And the Moon is at its edge.

Hark! hark! the thick black cloud is cleft,
    And the Moon is at its side:
Like waters shot from some high crag,
The lightning falls with never a jag
    A river steep and wide.

The strong wind reach'd the ship: it roar'd
    And dropp'd down, like a stone!
Beneath the lightning and the moon
    The dead men gave a groan.

They groan'd, they stirr'd, they all uprose,
    Ne spake, ne mov'd their eyes:
It had been strange, even in a dream
    To have seen those dead men rise.

The helmsman steerd, the ship mov'd on;
    Yet never a breeze up-blew;
The Marineres all 'gan work the ropes,
    Where they were wont to do:
They rais'd their limbs like lifeless tools –
    We were a ghastly crew.

The body of my brother's son
    Stood by me knee to knee:
The body and I pull'd at one rope,
    But he said nought to me –
And I quak'd to think of my own voice
    How frightful it would be!

The day-light dawn'd – they dropp'd their arms,
    And cluster'd round the mast:
Sweet sounds rose slowly thro' their mouths
    And from their bodies pass'd.

Around, around, flew each sweet sound,
    Then darted to the sun:
Slowly the sounds came back again
    Now mix'd, now one by one.

Sometimes a dropping from the sky
    I heard the Lavrock sing;
Sometimes all little birds that are
How they seem'd to fill the sea and air
    With their sweet jargoning,

And now 'twas like all instruments,
    Now like a lonely flute;
And now it is an angel's song
    That makes the heavens be mute.

It ceas'd: yet still the sails made on
    A pleasant noise till noon,
A noise like of a hidden brook
    In the leafy month of June,
That to the sleeping woods all night
    Singeth a quiet tune.

Listen, O listen, thou Wedding-guest!
    'Marinere! thou hast thy will:
'For that, which comes out of thine eye, doth make
    'My body and soul to be still.'

Never sadder tale was told
    To a man of woman born:
Sadder and wiser thou wedding-guest!
    Thou'lt rise to morrow morn.

Never sadder tale was heard
    By a man of woman born:
The Marineres all return'd to work
    As silent as beforne.

The Marineres all 'gan pull the ropes,
    But look at me they n'old:
Thought I, I am as thin as air –
    They cannot me behold.

Till noon we silently sail'd on
    Yet never a breeze did breathe:
Slowly and smoothly went the ship
    Mov'd onward from beneath.

Under the keel nine fathom deep
    From the land of mist and snow
The spirit slid: and it was He
    That made the Ship to go.
The sails at noon left off their tune
    And the Ship stood still also.

The sun right up above the mast
    Had fix'd her to the ocean:
But in a minute she 'gan stir
    With a short uneasy motion –
Backwards and forwards half her length
    With a short uneasy motion.

Then, like a pawing horse let go,
    She made a sudden bound:
It flung the blood into my head,
    And I fell into a swound.

74

How long in that same fit I lay,
    I have not to declare;
But ere my living life return'd,
I heard and in my soul discern'd
    Two voices in the air,

'Is it he? quoth one, 'Is this the man?
    'By him who died on cross,
'With his cruel bow he lay'd full low
    'The harmless Albatross.

'The spirit who 'bideth by himself
    'In the land of mist and snow,
'He lov'd the bird that lov'd the man
    'Who shot him with his bow.

The other was a softer voice,
    As soft as honey-dew:
Quoth he the man hath penance done,
    And penance more will do.

VI

First Voice
'But tell me, tell me! speak again,
    'Thy soft response renewing —
'What makes that ship drive on so fast?
    'What is the Ocean doing?

Second Voice
'Still as a Slave before his Lord,
    'The Ocean hath no blast:
'His great bright eye most silently
    'Up to the moon is cast —

'If he may know which way to go,
    'For she guides him smooth or grir
'See, brother, see! how graciously
    'She looketh down on him.

FIRST VOICE
'But why drives on that ship so fast
    'Withouten wave or wind?

SECOND VOICE
'The air is cut away before,
    'And closes from behind.

'Fly, brother, fly! more high, more high,
    'Or we shall be belated:
'For slow and slow that ship will go,
    'When the Marinere's trance is abated.'

I woke, and we were sailing on
    As in a gentle weather:
'Twas night, calm night, the moon was high;
    The dead men stood together.

All stood together on the deck,
    For a charnel-dungeon fitter:
All fix'd on me their stony eyes
    That in the moon did glitter.

The pang, the curse, with which they died,
    Had never pass'd away:
I could not draw my een from theirs
    Ne turn them up to pray.

And in its time the spell was snapt,
    And I could move my een:
I look'd far-forth, but little saw
    Of what might else be seen.

Like one, that on a lonely road
    Doth walk in fear and dread,
And having once turn'd round, walks on
    And turns no more his head:
Because he knows, a frightful fiend
    Doth close behind him tread.

But soon there breath'd a wind on me,
　Ne sound ne motion made:
Its path was not upon the sea
　In ripple or in shade.

It rais'd my hair, it fann'd my cheek,
　Like a meadow-gale of spring –
It mingled strangely with my fears,
　Yet it felt like a welcoming.

Swiftly, swiftly flew the ship,
　Yet she sail'd softly too:
Sweetly, sweetly blew the breeze –
　On me alone it blew.

O dream of joy! is this indeed
　The light-house top I see?
Is this the Hill? Is this the Kirk?
　Is this mine own countrée?

We drifted o'er the Harbour-bar,
　And I with sobs did pray –
'O let me be awake, my God!
　'Or let me sleep alway!'

The harbour-bay was clear as glass.
　So smoothly it was strewn!
And on the bay the moon light lay,
　And the shadow of the moon.

The moonlight bay was white all o'er,
　Till rising from the same,
Full many shapes, that shadows were,
　Like as of torches came.

A little distance from the prow
　Those dark-red shadows were;
But soon I saw that my own flesh
　Was red as in a glare.

I turn'd my head in fear and dread,
    And by the holy rood,
The bodies had advanc'd, and now
    Before the mast they stood.

They lifted up their stiff right arms,
    They held them strait and tight;
And each right-arm burnt like a torch,
    A torch that's borne upright.
Their stony eye-balls glitter'd on
    In the red and smoky light.

I pray'd and turn'd my head away
    Forth looking as before.
There was no breeze upon the bay,
    No wave against the shore.

The rock shone bright, the kirk no less
    That stands above the rock:
The moonlight steep'd in silentness
    The steady weathercock.

And the bay was white with silent light,
    Till rising from the same
Full many shapes, that shadows were,
    In crimson colours came.

A little distance from the prow
    Those crimson shadows were:
I turn'd my eyes upon the deck –
    O Christ! what saw I there?

Each corse lay flat, lifeless and flat;
    And by the Holy rood
A man all light, a seraph-man.
    On every corse there stood.

This seraph-band, each wav'd his hand:
    It was a heavenly sight:

They stood as signals to the land,
  Each one a lovely light:

This seraph-band, each wav'd his hand,
  No voice did they impart –
No voice; but O! the silence sank,
  Like music on my heart.

Eftsones I heard the dash of oars,
  I heard the pilot's cheer:
My head was turn'd perforce away
  And I saw a boat appear.

Then vanish'd all the lovely lights;
  The bodies rose anew:
With silence pace, each to his place,
  Came back the ghastly crew.
The wind, that shade nor motion made,
  On me alone it blew.

The pilot, and the pilot's boy
  I heard them coming fast:
Dear Lord in Heaven! it was a joy,
  The dead men could not blast.

I saw a third – I heard his voice:
  It is the Hermit good!
He singeth loud his godly hymns
  That he makes in the wood.
He'll shrieve my soul, he'll wash away
  The Albatross's blood.

VII

This Hermit good lives in that wood
  Which slopes down to the Sea.
How loudly his sweet voice he rears!
He loves to talk with Marineres
  That come from a far Contrée.

He kneels at morn and noon and eve –
    He hath a cushion plump:
It is the moss, that wholly hides
    The rotted old Oak-stump.

The Skiff-boat ne'rd: I heard them talk,
    'Why, this is strange, I trow!
'Where are those lights so many and fair
    'That signal made but now?

'Strange, by my faith! the Hermit said –
    'And they answer'd not our cheer.
'The planks look warp'd, and see those sails
    'How thin they are and sere!
'I never saw aught like to them
    'Unless perchance it were

'The skeletons of leaves that lag
    'My forest brook along:
'When the Ivy-tod is heavy with snow,
'And the Owlet whoops to the wolf below
    'That eats the she-wolf's young.

'Dear Lord! it has a fiendish look –
    (The Pilot made reply)
'I am a-fear'd. – 'Push on, push on!
    Said the Hermit cheerily.

The Boat came closer to the Ship,
    But I ne spake ne stirr'd!
The Boat came close beneath the Ship,
    And strait a sound was heard!

Under the water it rumbled on,
    Still louder and more dread:
It reach'd the Ship, it split the bay;
    The Ship went down like lead.

Stunn'd by that loud and dreadful sound,
    Which sky and ocean smote:
Like one that hath been seven days drown'd
    My body lay afloat:
But, swift as dreams, myself I found
    Within the Pilot's boat.

Upon the whirl, where sank the Ship,
    The boat spun round and round:
And all was still, save that the hill
    Was telling of the sound.

I mov'd my lips: the Pilot shriek'd
    And fell down in a fit.
The Holy Hermit rais'd his eyes
    And pray'd where he did sit.

I took the oars: the Pilot's boy,
    Who now doth crazy go,
Laugh'd loud and long, and all the while
    His eyes went to and fro,
'Ha! ha!' quoth he – 'full plain I see,
    'The devil knows how to row.'

And now all in mine own Countrée
    I stood on the firm land!
The Hermit stepp'd forth from the boat,
    And scarcely he could stand.

'O shrieve me, shrieve me, holy Man!
    The Hermit cross'd his brow –
'Say quick,' quoth he, 'I bid thee say
    'What manner man art thou?

Forthwith this frame of mine was wrench'd
    With a woeful agony,
Which forc'd me to begin my tale
    And then it left me free.

Since then at an uncertain hour,
    Now oftimes and now fewer,
That anguish comes and makes me tell
    My ghastly aventure.

I pass, like night, from land to land;
    I have strange power of speech;
The moment that his face I see
I know the man that must hear me;
    To him my tale I teach.

What loud uproar bursts from that door!
    The Wedding-guests are there;
But in the Garden-bower the Bride
    And Bride-maids singing are:
And hark the little Vesper-bell
    Which biddeth me to prayer.

O Wedding-guest! this soul hath been
    Alone on a wide wide sea:
So lonely 'twas, that God himself
    Scarce seemed there to be.

O sweeter than the Marriage-feast,
    'Tis sweeter far to me
To walk together to the Kirk
    With a goodly company.

To walk together to the Kirk
    And all together pray,
While each to his great father bends,
Old men, and babes, and loving friends,
    And Youths, and Maidens gay.

Farewell, farewell! but this I tell
    To thee, thou wedding guest!
He prayeth well who loveth well
    Both man and bird and beast.

He prayeth best who loveth best,
    All things both great and small:
For the dear God, who loveth us,
    He made and loveth all.

The Marinere, whose eye is bright,
    Whose beard with age is hoar,
Is gone; and now the wedding-guest
    Turn'd from the bridegroom's door.

He went, like one that hath been stunn'd
    And is of sense forlorn:
A sadder and a wiser man
    He rose the morrow morn.